Praise for *The Art and Busine*

"*The Art and Business of Teaching Yoga* (r
for self-care, personal practice, and inno
Enlightening and educational, this book
pandemic yoga, including marketing tips and advice on using social
media effectively. This book will help yoga teachers bring the magic of
yoga to the fore!" — **Maya Breuer**, yoga teacher (E-RYT 500)

"This much-needed resource lays out the fundamentals of teaching
yoga in a real and approachable way. You won't find any false promises
in *The Art and Business of Teaching Yoga*, and you will realize that, like
any other business, teaching yoga takes work, discipline, and diligence.
I thought I would never be interested in a 'business' book, but I picked
up this book and couldn't put it down. It is a great read from start to
finish." — **Colleen Saidman Yee**, author of *Yoga for Life*

"Making a living as a yoga teacher requires entrepreneurial vision and
business insight. In addition to helping teachers become more skillful
with their craft, *The Art and Business of Teaching Yoga* demystifies the
business and marketing landscape of being a yoga professional — subjects that nearly every yoga professional can use more support with.
This book will now be required reading for all my teacher training
programs!" — **Jason Crandell**, master yoga teacher trainer

"Amy and Taro are here to help you grow your teaching with care and
poise. With guidance on everything from choosing your teaching medium, building content, and creating compelling sequences to prioritizing your personal practice, this book walks you through the shift
from in-person to virtual teaching and beyond." — **Elena Brower**,
bestselling author of *Practice You* and *Softening Time*

"The modern transformation of yoga over the past fifty years has caused
us to rethink its definition, purpose, and meaning. Amy Ippoliti and
Taro Smith provide indispensable guidance for any student, teacher,
or businessperson who aims to understand yoga then and now. Their
hard-won experience, integrity, and insight are applied to yoga's complex history, theory, and practice. Both accurate and accessible, this
is the book to read if you want to teach yoga in the modern world of
business — and understand how business is yet another kind of yoga."
— **Dr. Douglas R. Brooks**, professor of religion,
University of Rochester, Rochester, New York

"This comprehensive guide empowers yoga enthusiasts with essential insights and strategies for a fulfilling journey in the world of yoga instruction. May the words on these pages inspire you to embark on or continue your journey as a beacon of light, illuminating minds and nurturing spirits along the way." — **Koya Webb**, author of *Let Your Fears Make You Fierce* and founder of Get Loved Up yoga school

"This comprehensive book is an essential resource for any yoga teacher who is ready to take their teaching game and business acumen to the next level. Whether you're brand new to teaching or a seasoned veteran, you will learn how to ensure you are working wisely, efficiently, and effectively in growing your life and career!" — **Hawah Kasat**, founder of One Common Unity

"*The Art of Business and Teaching Yoga* (revised) is an essential guide to crafting a teaching practice that is authentic and of service to both the times and your students. This labor of love is transformational and practical, covering the full spectrum of everything you need to know to be a successful teacher technically, financially, and spiritually." — **Reggie Hubbard**, activist, strategist, and chief serving officer of Active Peace Yoga

"Amy Ippoliti and Taro Smith are the ultimate power duo when it comes to combining the worlds of yoga, teaching, and business. I'm so happy to have their voice encouraging teachers to expand intelligently and thoughtfully." — **Kathryn Budig**, author of *Aim True* and *The Women's Health Big Book of Yoga*

"Amy Ippoliti's teaching style has had a profound impact on my home yoga practice, and I'm excited to see how this text transforms my yoga teaching practice!" — **Jessamyn Stanley**, international yoga teacher and author of *Every Body Yoga* and *Yoke*

"Amy Ippoliti and Taro Smith are expertly qualified to enlighten aspiring and experienced yoga teachers on how to thrive as a teacher, while ensuring that they honor their life outside of the profession. Get ready to make your mark; *The Art and Business of Teaching Yoga* is the comprehensive, nuts-and-bolts guide for a sustainable, successful, and fulfilling yoga teaching career." — **Rod Stryker**, author of *The Four Desires* and founder of ParaYoga

The Art and Business
of Teaching Yoga

The Art and Business of Teaching Yoga

The Yoga Professional's Guide to a Fulfilling Career

REVISED EDITION

AMY IPPOLITI AND TARO SMITH, PhD

New World Library
Novato, California

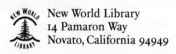

New World Library
14 Pamaron Way
Novato, California 94949

The material in this book is intended for educational purposes only. No expressed or implied guarantee of the effects of the use of the recommendations can be given or liability taken.

Text design by Tona Pearce Myers

Library of Congress Cataloging-in-Publication Data is available.

Names: Ippoliti, Amy, author.
Title: The art and business of teaching yoga : the yoga professional's guide to a fulfilling career / Amy Ippoliti and Taro Smith, PhD.
Description: Revised edition. | Novato, California : New World Library, 2023. | Includes index. | Summary: "The definitive guide to flourishing as a yoga instructor, expanded and updated with guidance on how to adapt to the post-pandemic teaching landscape. The book is written for yoga teachers in all stages of their career, from newly certified beginners to experienced professionals looking to expand their businesses"-- Provided by publisher.
Identifiers: LCCN 2023040820 (print) | LCCN 2023040821 (ebook) | ISBN 9781608688784 | ISBN 9781608688791 (ebook)
Subjects: LCSH: Yoga--Study and teaching. | BISAC: HEALTH & FITNESS / Yoga. | BUSINESS & ECONOMICS / Entrepreneurship. | BUSINESS & ECONOMICS / Skills. | BUSINESS & ECONOMICS / Training.
Classification: LCC RA781.67 .I77 2023 (print) | LCC RA781.67 (ebook) | DDC 613.7/046076--dc23/eng/20230921
LC record available at https://lccn.loc.gov/2023040820
LC ebook record available at https://lccn.loc.gov/2023040821

First printing of revised edition, December 2023
ISBN 978-1-60868-878-4
Ebook ISBN 978-1-60868-879-1
Printed in Canada on 100% postconsumer-waste recycled paper

New World Library is proud to be a Gold Certified Environmentally Responsible Publisher. Publisher certification awarded by Green Press Initiative.

10   9   8   7   6   5   4   3   2

*In a world desperate for more love, compassion,
and connection, this book is dedicated to all yoga teachers —
past, present, and future — who serve as
community leaders, heroes, and mentors.
Your gifts are helping to make a better world
and a more livable future.*

Contents

Preface to the Revised Edition   xi

Introduction   I

Part I: Becoming a Yoga Teacher

Chapter 1: Teaching Today   7

Chapter 2: Presenting Yourself as a Teacher   21

Part II: Getting Down to Business

Chapter 3: Yoga Business Basics   47

Chapter 4: Online Yoga Business Basics   69

Chapter 5: Building Your Business   107

Chapter 6: Marketing Your Business   123

Chapter 7: Social Media   137

Chapter 8: Forming Good Professional Relationships   159

Chapter 9: Managing Your Business Finances   165

Part III: Teaching Well

Chapter 10: Class Planning and Preparation   173

Chapter 11: Teaching In-Person Classes Skillfully   197

Chapter 12: Teaching Online Skillfully   211

Part IV: Leading by Example

Chapter 13: Self-Care   241
Chapter 14: Leadership and Karma Yoga
    (Regenerative Practices and Social Change)   251

Conclusion: Light Up the World   271
Acknowledgments   273
Index   275
About the Authors   289

Preface to the Revised Edition

Originally published in 2016, *The Art and Business of Teaching Yoga* immediately became the essential resource for those looking to start or maintain a successful career as a yoga instructor. The first edition not only covered how to be a better teacher, but also helped readers successfully navigate the ins and outs of small (or not-so-small) business ownership.

A few short years later, the landscape has changed drastically. The pandemic of 2020 drove a surge of online (digital) yoga. Yoga enthusiasts got used to the convenience, time saving, and lower cost of practicing at home. Though they are missing out on some of the benefits of in-person yoga (hands-on assists, community, and being seen in 3D), many don't want to stop practicing online. Digital yoga, it seems, is here to stay. Also, yoga teachers are now facing broad cultural shifts, economic uncertainty, social changes, and an evolving environmental crisis. To succeed in this new landscape, teachers will need to know how to serve more compassionately, improve their leadership and community-building skills, teach yoga skillfully, and carve out a business that meets the trying times in which we find ourselves.

This revised edition shares new insights on building an online yoga business, offers quick tips for teaching yoga effectively online, and explores the practice of karma yoga (the yoga of action and service) and how yoga teachers can better address the challenges of our time.

Introduction

As a teen in the mid-eighties, I took my first
yoga class before sticky mats existed. I read the *Tao Te Ching*,
volunteered with environmental organizations, and spent my
summers immersed in nature, community, and marching on
Washington for animal rights and the environment.

I became a yoga teacher at age twenty-seven, after eleven
years of strictly asana practice. I knew that there was much
more to yoga than just physical postures. Though I felt too
young and unqualified to be a yoga teacher, my teacher, Cyndi
Lee, had just started training teachers and welcomed me once
I'd gathered the courage to apply to her training.

That first training satisfied my craving to understand even
just a fraction of the infinite mystery of yoga. And through
Cyndi's belief in me, I felt brave enough to become a teacher.

After the training, I started hanging out with other yogins* who shared similar values. They too preferred to live
in rhythm with nature, to be aware in their bodies, and to be
mindful about how their choices affected the earth. As we

---

* *Yogin* is a gender-neutral term meaning "yoga practitioner."

practiced more and more yoga, our sensitivity to everything in the world around us increased: to our relationships with our loved ones, to food, to strangers, and to how we chose to spend our money.

Back then, a career as a yoga teacher was unheard-of. Until the mid-nineties, many people thought of yoga teachers as super-far-out whack-a-doodles who led classes in their darkened living rooms on thick red shag carpets, with incense and candles burning. People my age were supposed to join the "real" world of nine-to-five work and responsibility. I tried — and failed — to get with this program. I wanted more time for reflection and study, more flexibility (pardon the pun) with my schedule, and the companionship of others who shared my ideals. And I also very much wanted to help others feel and be their best selves.

So I forged ahead as a newbie instructor, joining the small force of yoga teachers trying hard to find teaching opportunities. This was the nineties in New York City, and practicing yoga was still on the fringe.

Sometime in 1998, yoga hit mainstream culture. Word spread that people like Sting and Madonna had a yoga practice. I suddenly went from scrambling for jobs to turning down teaching opportunities because my schedule was booked solid. Suddenly yoga was all the rage.

What could be better? More people doing yoga meant more people learning and growing in ways that could only increase peace and harmony in the world, right?

But popularization always brings challenges along with benefits. Longtime yoga practitioners debated whether age-old ideas were being diluted to appeal to the masses or adapted to serve teachers' personal agendas. Were people being attracted to yoga for dubious reasons? In addition, yoga's adoption by celeb-rities seemed to imply that it was an elitist, exclusive practice.

As I wrestled with those questions, while teaching and training other teachers, I became acutely aware of how diffi-cult it is to maintain one's own practice, study, and passion while also managing to make a decent living.

Fast-forward to 2010, when I met Taro Smith through a mu-tual friend. He was an entrepreneur specializing in lifestyle- and wellness-oriented businesses. He was also a trained yoga teacher who understood teachers and their struggles to earn a liveli-hood. He was, and is, smart, enthusiastic, and inspiring.

To help the best and most dedicated teachers succeed in the now-crowded marketplace, with Taro's help I developed an online course for yoga teachers. It presented ways for teachers to take back time on their mat, build a strong student base, become more financially stable, serve their yoga students in fresh and exciting ways, and inspire even more students to embrace yoga.

Taro and I were very aware that most yoga teachers aren't MBAs. And while any small-business operator can pick up a how-to manual online or in a bookstore, we knew that yoga professionals needed guidance that aligned with the values of yoga.

In just a year and a half, we trained over fifteen hundred teachers in forty-three different countries all over the world. When our training bore fruit and yoga teachers started get-ting results in their communities, we established our company, 90 Monkeys, now Vesselify. It is dedicated to offering a solid online and in-person education resource for yoga teachers, with a full curriculum of professional development courses.

Our "90 Minutes to Change the World" course formed the

basis for much of the content of this book. Taro and I wrote the book together, but for simplicity's sake, we opted to write it from the perspective of "I," Amy. It empowers teachers to develop yoga-specific career skills, including ways to:

- increase class attendance
- inspire students
- establish and maintain a great reputation
- sustain their own teaching with ongoing education and practice
- forge mutually beneficial relationships with others in the community

Following the assessments, exercises, and approaches in this book can help you increase your satisfaction in teaching yoga, the amount you are earning, and the number of people you are reaching. And if you are a new teacher, starting out with this knowledge will save you from missteps.

There is no magic button to push to become the perfect yoga teacher or operator of the ideal yoga business. You have to work at it. As yoga lovers and yoga teachers, Taro and I know what that means, and we'll walk you through the steps that will benefit and sustain both you and your students.

We believe in the power of yoga to help people live mindful, happy lives, and we know from personal experience that teaching yoga offers both teacher and student life-changing, life-enhancing benefits. This book will show you how to share those benefits with others most effectively.

Part I

BECOMING A YOGA TEACHER

CHAPTER ONE

Teaching Today

Millions of people have experienced yoga's benefits. Some have found that it lessens pain or stress, and some have incorporated yoga into their meditation or spiritual practice. Many others find that yoga just *feels* good and increases their overall sense of well-being.

Yoga has traditionally been seen as a path to heightened consciousness and mindfulness, though this aspect is increasingly less emphasized in the West. The practice facilitates a profound awareness of how body, mind, and spirit are linked and how each individual is connected to all life on the planet.

In a world dominated by nonstop activity and the proliferation of high-tech devices, yoga is one of the few popular endeavors that require only a sticky mat and a commitment to practice. No technology is needed.

As a yoga practitioner, you know that yoga practice is sometimes the only time of day when someone truly unplugs, enters a state of calm, moves their body, and simply breathes. As a yoga teacher, you have the honor and privilege of guiding people through that process — a process that is sometimes delightful and often challenging, but always rewarding.

Teaching yoga is often thought of as a lifestyle business. This means that you have chosen a pastime that is central to your own lifestyle and are taking the chance that you can create a career, or supplement other income, by devoting yourself to it.

We are called to teach because we love any excuse to get on our yoga mats, cherish watching our students develop, and likely have a pronounced aversion to cubicle life, endless meetings, and uncomfortable shoes!

The Good News about Teaching Yoga Today

Yoga Journal and Yoga Alliance, the professional organization representing yoga teachers, studios, and schools, conducted an extensive study into the state of yoga in the United States.* According to their 2016 "Yoga in America" report, 36.7 million people practiced yoga, up from 20.4 million in 2012. Yoga is not only growing, it's booming. In fact, 28 percent of all Americans reported taking a yoga class at some point in their lives. More men and more older people are practicing than ever before: in 2015, there were approximately 10 million male practitioners and almost 14 million practitioners over the age of fifty. Surely these numbers have only grown since 2016.

Yogins are also contributing to the economy, spending over $16 billion annually on classes, yoga clothing, equipment, and accessories, up from $10 billion in 2012. Evidently, yoga is enticing: 34 percent of Americans say they are somewhat likely or very likely to practice yoga in the next twelve months — which is equal to more than 80 million Americans. Why

---

* The full study results are available at https://www.yogaalliance.org /2016YogaInAmericaStudy.

do they want to try yoga? They reported wanting to increase their flexibility, relieve stress, and improve their fitness levels.

According to the survey, yoga is an increasing part of life in the United States. Between 2012 and 2016, the percentage of Americans aware of yoga jumped from 75 percent to 90 percent. One in three Americans reported trying yoga on their own (not in a class) at least once.

The findings also indicate that yoga practitioners tend to have a positive self-image: they are 20 percent more likely than nonpractitioners to report that they have "good balance," "good physical agility or dexterity," or "good range of motion or flexibility" or that they "give back to the community."

The study also shows that yoga students are highly concerned about their health, their community, and the environment. More than 50 percent of practitioners report trying to eat sustainable foods and live green, compared with about a third of the general population. Nearly half of yoga practitioners report donating time to their communities, compared with just 26 percent of those who don't practice yoga.

Perhaps not surprisingly, yoga teachers and teacher trainees are even more tuned in to environmental and social issues and to living and eating consciously than other yoga practitioners: 22 percent of yoga teachers and trainees are vegetarians, compared with 8 percent of other yoga practitioners and 3 percent of the general public; and 60 percent of yoga teachers and trainees use natural health and beauty products, compared with 44 percent of other yoga practitioners and 21 percent of the general public.

Statistics like these support what has always been true in the yoga circles in which I run: yogins are living life with more self-awareness and positive self-regard, and as a result of this increased sensitivity, they are making an encouraging differ-ence for the environment and in their communities.

What does all this mean for you as a teacher or aspiring teacher? The demand for yoga teachers is higher than ever — and unlikely to decrease anytime soon.

The Challenges of Being a Yoga Teacher

With statistics like those above, it's clear that as a yoga teacher, you're part of a movement that is growing exponentially and one that is becoming more and more a part of life in our soci-ety. As exciting as this can be, it's important to recognize that there are also challenges that come along with becoming or being a teacher. This book will help you understand and min-imize these challenges, see how they apply to your specific sit-uation, and find ways to manage them with skill and finesse.

First, with the growing popularity of yoga, the demand for teacher training has created a small army of yoga teachers all over the world, and you are just one of them. It's not as easy to stand out as it used to be.

At the same time, because of this popularity, modern yoga is sometimes criticized as being overly commercialized. Aware-ness of these criticisms can make it difficult to feel confident promoting yourself, spreading the word about your teaching, or asking to be compensated for your time and energy.

What's more, even though you have probably invested lots of time and money in developing your yoga education, teach-ing yoga has not traditionally been a lucrative career.

Yoga and Money

The ethical aspects of combining yoga with business, money, and marketing can be troubling: 50 percent of yoga teachers polled in our courses reported feeling awkward about charging for their teaching. But a great many of these teachers reported that they felt uncomfortable because of what *other* people think about yoga and money.

The reality is that yoga means different things to different people. Here are three common categories or belief systems:

1. Those who think that yoga should maintain its roots solely in an esoteric and spiritual practice and are therefore more likely to have a hard time with the commercial side of yoga and its marketing and promotion.

2. Those who see yoga teaching as a hobby or side job. These yogins are usually fortunate enough to be able to teach without worrying about compensation.

3. Those who live fully in the twenty-first-century, modern world and see teaching yoga as a profession through which they earn a living.

If you're serious about teaching yoga as an occupation, I'd like to help you understand why the third category is the clear choice and how the other two belief systems can confuse the profession of teaching yoga.

SHOULD YOGA BE FREE?

Every time a teacher offers a yoga class for free (or teaches for very little) they are *paying* to teach that class. They bought the gas for their car to get there, they paid for parking outside the studio, and potentially they rented the space too. Even a virtual class has overhead, such as equipment, online meeting subscription fees, and more. In other words, the teacher spent more money than they earned. Whenever a class is given away, that choice influences the market, thereby undermining others who depend on their teaching income to support themselves. I almost never teach for free, and when I do it's typically for a benefit in which participants have donated to the cause. It's fine to teach for free once in a while, but be mindful not to make this your modus operandi.

Yoga is now a $16 billion industry in the United States. Marketing of yoga accessories — everything from mats, props, and bags to yoga-specific clothing and even jewelry and nutritional supplements — has exploded. Promoters organize yoga conferences and festivals with lots of tangentially related activities, such as music concerts, slacklining, Hula-Hooping, stand-up paddleboarding, and even wine tasting. With the promotional efforts that accompany these enterprises, criticism is inevitable.

For yoga teachers thinking of yoga as both a practice and a profession, it's helpful to understand the current state of affairs, and also to know a little of the history of yoga in both India and the West. Yoga practice and teaching in the West have been heavily influenced by particular schools of yoga with a focus on spiritual enlightenment — the traditions of Patanjali's classical yoga and Advaita Vedanta — using yoga to transcend our identification with the material world. Practitioners of these forms of yoga renounced material wealth and other forms of indulgence, many taking vows of celibacy. But these schools of yoga and their philosophies are not the only ones; they just happen to be the forms that gained an early foothold in the West. As a result, the yoga world is dealing with the residual effects of this one outlook.

MONEY AND YOGA IN THE DISTANT PAST

Once upon a more patriarchal time, thousands of years ago in India, the teacher-student relationship was focused on *dakshina* (the sacred compensation or sacrifice), rooted in the notion that the student, in complete deference to the teacher, would pay whatever fee the teacher demanded. The demand was not always explicit, just assumed. The patriarchal model was guru above, student below.

In the West, education and the teacher-student relationship are based more on parity than on hierarchy or authority. For yoga in the West, and yoga in the twenty-first century, a new paradigm is required.

Those who object to treating yoga as a business perhaps fail to consider that yoga is not solely a spiritual practice: it is a form of education, encompassing physical activity, wellness, philosophy, and even history. And if yoga is a multifaceted form of education rather than an esoteric spiritual quest, it stands to reason that, as with other forms of training, such as piano lessons or a language course, a yoga education costs money. It is time for a more modern paradigm in the West, one that regards teaching yoga, like other forms of schooling, as a legitimate profession.

While sleazy marketing is unattractive in any field, and particularly in yoga, yoga cannot be kept free of promotion or commerce. If yoga teachers do not promote the merits of yoga and their own expertise in teaching it, then how will people find the path to those benefits? The great rewards of yoga are worth sharing with the world. The distinctive gifts that yoga teachers can offer their students are worth publicizing, and in our modern world they have monetary value.

It might help to apply some fundamental yoga philosophy to the controversy. *The Yoga Sutras of Patanjali* (second century CE) discusses two concepts for explaining reality: *prakriti* and *purusha*.

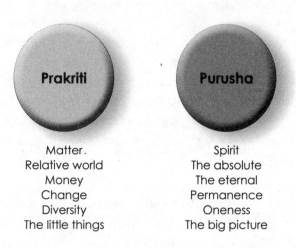

Prakriti	Purusha
Matter	Spirit
Relative world	The absolute
Money	The eternal
Change	Permanence
Diversity	Oneness
The little things	The big picture

Prakriti encompasses matter, the material world, feelings and emotions, anything that changes, diversity, and the "little things," including money. *Purusha* encompasses spirit, the absolute, the eternal, that which does not change.

Purusha-prioritizing traditions see the material world as a problem to be fixed or to withdraw from. Sayings such as "I am not this body, I am not this mind" and "All of that is an illusion" come from a school identified with *purusha*. Strict followers attempt to suppress their feelings, stanch desire, conquer the human ego, and retreat from the real world through meditation in order to attain the beautiful vision of *purusha*. An exclusive focus on other-than-the-world makes it difficult to negotiate our twenty-first-century sphere.

There is an alternative view that embraces both *prakriti* and *purusha*. It is embodied in the Tantric schools of yoga, which are not as well known in the West. Tantra has come to be thought of as being all about sexuality, but it is actually a much broader body of yoga and philosophy, one that addresses all aspects of human life. (To learn more about the origins of Tantra, we recommend *The Origins of Yoga and Tantra* by Geoffrey Samuel or *The Alchemical Body* by David G. White.)

Embracing both *prakriti* and *purusha* allows us to acknowledge that there are mouths to feed, worthy organizations working to make a difference that need our support, bills to pay, and kids to put through college. None of this is illusory; it is real.

Dichotomies that characterize yoga as beautiful and consumerism as ugly are neither helpful nor realistic. In fact, there is no escaping consumerism through yoga; humans, like everything else in the food chain, must eat and consume resources. The more interesting and important question is, How can we create a paradigm for thinking about money and consumerism that is ethical, conscious, and sustainable?

The Vicious Cycle of Yoga Teaching

I started the "90 Minutes" course because I knew what a privilege it is to teach yoga and live the lifestyle of a yogin. However, as a trainer of yoga teachers and a teacher myself, I was witnessing firsthand the struggles we went through to make ends meet. Over and over I saw teachers in what I came to call the "vicious cycle of yoga teaching." It goes like this:

1. Run all over town teaching eighteen or more classes a week to make ends meet.
2. Oops, no time for your own practice! No time to plan classes!
3. Teach subpar class because of lack of practice, inspiration, or groundedness.
4. Get home, have no time for reflection, fun, recreation, or family.
5. Get up the next day with even less inspiration, and teach to a dwindling number of students.
6. Make insufficient money to pay bills, afford necessary continuing education, or have much-needed free time.
7. Repeat.

Seeing good teachers teaching too many classes per week in order to pay bills and with no time or money for continuing education is painful. Many injure themselves during demonstrations because they have not been able to give time to their own practice and therefore stay strong in their bodies. Their classes and students inevitably suffer as a result.

Witnessing the graduates of my teacher trainings struggling to such a severe degree led me to put as much time into studying business as I had put into studying yoga philosophy. I wanted to help other yoga teachers, and by extension their students, by teaching them professional business practices.

Studying business and marketing gave me valuable tools, and it also taught me that there are two realities you need to face as a yoga teacher. Here they are, along with my suggestions for navigating them:

1. Most American full-time yoga teachers fall into the vicious cycle, especially new ones. Some teachers manage to avoid it, but given the changing nature of the market, there's no guarantee that you will be able to. I suggest that you keep this reality in mind and try to avoid falling into the cycle to the best of your ability, by not teaching more classes than you can happily handle (see pages 114–20) and by building your own practice time into your schedule every week.

2. We cannot control the market because there will always be yoga teachers willing to work for very little — since either they are new and eager to work or they are treating their teaching as a hobby. The choice to teach for less than market value unfortunately devalues the services all yoga professionals offer, so ultimately we must make the best of what the market will bear. The good news is that the more educated you are about professional business practices, the more likely it is that the market will reward you.

Your practice, your teaching, and your classes all benefit from your ability to view yoga as a valuable profession in today's world. Your students need you to be as skillful at life's practicalities as you are on the mat. As I hope is now clear, yoga and everyday life actually can't be separated.

TEACHER TRAINING

In addition to being able to teach a sequence of poses, yoga teachers would be wise to have an education in yoga alignment, therapeutic application, and the rich history and philosophy of yoga. Typically, based on Yoga Alliance standards, two hundred hours is the minimum adequate training time, with five hundred hours being the pinnacle of training. In some ways these numbers are arbitrary. Teaching yoga, like the practice of yoga, is a lifelong endeavor, and as such, continuing education and being a student for the long haul are essential to teaching yoga well.

Training programs vary from trainer to trainer and from school to school. Furthermore, some styles of yoga emphasize alignment, form, and philosophy more than others do.

You need teacher trainers who have been well trained themselves. Ask your teacher or program coordinator the following questions:

- Are you a graduate of a 200-hour or 500-hour training?
- Are you a graduate of more than one teacher training program?
- Did the style of yoga you trained in emphasize alignment and form? Philosophy?
- Who are your teachers? Are your trainers known for working with students on form, alignment, and injury prevention during the practice?
- Do you have any other credentials, such as being a licensed physical therapist or massage therapist or having a sports medicine background?

The Full Scope of Teaching Yoga Today

Yoga classes are often a refuge for students, a rare and precious place of quiet, reflection, and connection with self and with community. The spaces where we teach can often feel sacred, places where something special happens. But we aren't preachers or gurus. We don't tell others what to believe.

What we do is teach asana, a physical practice, informed by years of tradition and philosophy. We are in the business of offering a path to spiritual health and wellness. The multifaceted nature of our endeavor (art and profession, involving body, mind, and spirit) may strike some as paradoxical, but this multifaceted, twenty-first-century educational paradigm is empowering. Embrace it.

CHAPTER TWO

Presenting Yourself as a Teacher

Longtime yogins are accustomed to self-awareness, self-inquiry, and self-assessment. These skills are also vitally important to yoga teachers. Yes, we must understand our students' expectations and motivations (and we'll discuss how to do that), but we can't thrive without understanding our own expectations and motivations or without having a clear awareness of our strengths and weaknesses.

I suggest you assess yourself in three categories: skilled yoga teacher, exemplary yoga teacher, and successful yoga teacher. This process will reveal your assets and deficiencies, as well as the actions you can take to improve. It will also help you develop a fuller and richer understanding of exactly why and how you teach.

What do I mean by *skilled*, *exemplary*, and *successful*? Here's how I define these terms for yoga teachers:

Skilled: Skilled at teaching, competent
Exemplary: Able to serve as a role model and example
  for others
Successful: Fulfilling personal career goals and making
  a comfortable living financially

This is not a progression. I don't mean that you should first work toward being skilled and then, once you've achieved that, move on to becoming exemplary. And, to be clear, I'm not suggesting that success will inevitably follow from being skilled and exemplary. What's more, none of these objectives is necessarily better than the others. The most skilled teachers may not be the best role models. Wonderful role models may not be the most successful teachers. You could reach your own personal career goals with gaps in your skills.

What I mean is that you should strive to attain a balance among all these objectives. When someone asks if you are a skilled teacher, an exemplary one, or a successful one, it is possible to say, "All of the above!"

We'll examine each category more closely now, and the remainder of the book is also loosely organized around these categories. Part II, "Getting Down to Business," covers the successful category. Part III, "Teaching Well," explains in detail how to be a skilled teacher. Finally, part IV, "Leading by Example," covers the components of being an exemplary teacher.

The Skilled Yoga Teacher

Skilled yoga teachers are those who know their stuff. They have been well trained and mentored by an experienced teacher, strive to remain current, and maintain a regular practice of their own. Because they understand alignment, they can offer effective verbal instruction and hands-on assists. Their competence allows them to embody what they are teaching.

Skilled teachers offer a balance in the amount of instruction they offer — not too much, nor too little, but just enough. They understand the importance of silence. They prepare for their classes and observe their students well enough to teach the students who are actually in the room, even if this means altering their prepared class plan.

Skilled teachers produce good results because they meet students where they are, while also inspiring joyful perseverance. They look for and acknowledge progress rather than perfection. And they offer the kind of verbal cues and demonstrations that allow students to experience tangible shifts in their bodies.

Finally, skilled teachers manage class time well. They begin and end on time and balance the amount of time spent holding on the left and right sides, and on practicing standing poses and inversions, for example. (Teachers are not inherently better than students at managing time, so watch the clock or use a stopwatch in your preparations if necessary.)

The Not-So-Skilled Teacher

To get crystal clear about what makes a skilled teacher, it can be helpful to look at a few counterexamples. One flaw is expecting a student to be someone they are not or inflating a student's expectations beyond safe levels. Or a teacher might have insightful things to say but deliver them in a boring monotone. Unskilled teachers might also make students feel inferior, small, or talked down to. An unskilled teacher might make grandiose claims, like the ability to diagnose and cure a student's ailment. Worse yet, an unskilled teacher might convey the attitude that it's "my way or the highway."

The Exemplary Yoga Teacher

I define this type of teacher as a role model and example for others. They are both inspirational and down-to-earth. They have boundaries but are also available. They are authentic and so encourage students to be themselves as well. They follow a code of ethics that helps them move in the world with sensitivity and consideration for others and a high regard for the teacher-student relationship (see more on yoga teacher ethics in the section below). This teacher embraces collaboration with colleagues and is community oriented. With students and colleagues, and in the larger community, they embody warmth and caring.

Despite these almost saintly qualities, an exemplary teacher is relentlessly real — honest, trustworthy, and fair. (This teacher understands that they are being paid and so want their students to get extra value for their money.) While some students may want to place this teacher on a pedestal and view them as somehow superhuman, the teacher does not allow it. (Exemplary teachers want to be on mats, not on pedestals!) Without being falsely self-deprecating, an exemplary teacher acknowledges their own foibles. While confident in their role as teacher, they are also always learning and sometimes struggling. It's not a weakness to acknowledge difficulty; in fact, it can be a bridge to greater connection.

Modern Ethics: Beyond the Yamas and Niyamas

Almost every yoga teacher training program has a section on ethics, specifically the *yamas* and *niyamas* as outlined in Patanjali's *Yoga Sutras*. Ethics are particularly important in the teacher-student relationship in yoga because students may be vulnerable when they come to us for practice. It's vital that we instill their trust in us as professionals. A natural power differential is inherent in the teacher-student relationship. Therefore, we teachers need to be extra accountable as role models and hold ourselves to high standards. To read more about conduct and ethics pertaining to the teacher-student relationship,

Google the "California Yoga Teachers Association Code of Conduct," which was written by veteran teacher Judith Hanson Lasater in 1995.

The *yamas* and *niyamas*, the first and second limbs of Patanjali's eight limbs of yoga, are the pragmatic principles and "rules" that were created to guide people's actions given the karmic, or cause-and-effect, nature of the world. In that karmic world we need human decency and accountability.

But karma isn't the whole picture. Its opposite is known as *lila*. *Lila* encompasses divine play, vulnerability, ambiguity, and the fact that anything can happen. As humans we are vulnerable to what the world dishes out, and the future is uncertain and unpredictable.

The *yamas* and *niyamas* are important and straightforward, and yet they don't quite account for a world that is also *lilic*. In one moment your life could be calm, and in the next breath it could change forever if a family member is hit by a car, your spouse gets laid off, or your health takes a turn for the worse.

Don't get me wrong — the *yamas* and *niyamas* are essential, and I wouldn't want to live in the world without them. Yet it's important to recognize that they originated as part of an ascetical paradigm meant to encourage seekers to move away from the world of social contracts.

Most third graders have been taught the equivalent of the *yamas* and *niyamas* ("don't steal," "give credit where it is due," "don't lie," "be clean," etc.) and learned to follow them. As yoga teachers we are ready for more. It is time to take ethics one step further and into modern times. We can do this by recognizing that we live in a world that is both karmic (predictable) and *lilic* (unpredictable). To put it plainly, having modern ethics means having your "ducks in a row" or having your act together. It means creating basic stability in your life so that when *lila* happens you can roll with the play of the universe rather than getting run over by it. Being prepared for any possibility means that you can create opportunities out of challenges rather than being a victim to them.

Why is this approach more ethical? Because when your life falls apart and you're not prepared, your problems inevitably become other people's problems. Take, for example, the yoga teacher who kept putting off getting health insurance until one day she was diagnosed with a serious health issue requiring extensive surgery. To cover her medical bills, the community had to rally to put together benefit classes and raise funds on her behalf. Or the person who put off getting snow tires on his car and then got stuck in the snow, blocking a family's driveway. Now he not only had let his coworkers down because he couldn't get to work but also impacted the four people in the house, who were now unable to get on with their day! Examples like these are endless.

Another thing to consider is this: if the *yamas* and *niyamas* are part of a yoga teacher's curriculum, why do we see so many yoga teachers breaking ethical contracts and lacking professional responsibility?

Herein lies the problem. If ethics exist only in a karmic world that yogins are aiming to escape from, then they can easily blame their "elevated state" as the reason for their violating ethical standards. In short, the guru gets a pass. A teacher who blames their transgressions or lack of responsibility on their spirituality is doing what is called "spiritual bypassing."

Modern, professional, and ethical teachers are, in Sanskrit, *auchitya*: "filled with appropriateness." They demonstrate awareness and understand the world they live in. In summary, these teachers:

- understand the features of a social contract (*yamas* and *niyamas*) and know that they are not exempt from its precepts.
- are functional and stable in their embodied life. How? By inviting vulnerability (*lila*) rather than being victimized by it.
- can embrace the paradox of social contract (karma) and divine play (*lila*).
- have their act together!

The more of an authority you are in your field, and the more privileges you receive because of that authority, the more accountable and responsible you have to be. The best leaders surround themselves with a system of checks and balances — or a high council to advise them on decisions and to call them out when they're buying into their own hype. These leaders are able to take feedback well and openly seek guidance from others.

Take some time to think about your life and how you can increase stability and harness a system of checks and balances. Some ideas include hiring a therapist, putting a studio manager in place, seeking the support of a mentor or friends who can be frank with you, having an attorney you can call upon on short notice, assembling a business team, having godparents for your children, setting up retirement and contingency funds, having life insurance, staying on top of car maintenance, seeking help from family, having a list of pet sitters you can call on, and lining up a team of health professionals for you and your family.

A Word on Charisma

While exemplary teachers are humble, they also have a presence. Some would call this charisma. Although charisma might seem like a quality you have to be born with, everyone has a spark inside. It's just a matter of uncovering your light and letting it shine.

Martha Beck wrote a fantastic article on her belief that everyone (wallflowers included) has an innate and intangible "It" factor. As an example, she used the celebrity beagle Uno, the first of his breed to win the prestigious Westminster Kennel Club Dog Show in 2008.* In her article Beck points out that despite being a beagle, often considered less interesting than more exotic breeds, this particular dog charmed the crowd and won the show with a standing ovation. She described how Uno shone his attention on everyone around him and how he exuded confidence, owned the ring, and held an elegant posture with ease.

There are many ways to unveil your natural charisma. Simple steps include making eye contact, standing and sitting up straight, speaking a bit more quickly, and mirroring the other person's body language when you're in conversation. However, having charisma mostly comes from "owning" your own space while turning your attention toward others. People pay attention to the person who is paying attention to them!

Having charisma is not inauthentic. It isn't an attempt to dazzle or garner adoration. Instead it is motivated by the teacher's genuine desire to optimize their ability to educate and be of service. It's a way of connecting.

The Not-So-Exemplary Teacher

Not-so-exemplary teachers may be talented and have much to offer as role models but may hold themselves back and get in

---

*   See https://www.oprah.com/spirit/charisma-and-self-confidence -martha-becks-strategy.

their own way, meaning that instead of trusting themselves, they become mired in self-doubt or negative self-talk.

Unfortunately, not all yoga teachers are well prepared to serve and give value to students. In some cases, a teacher tries too hard to make a good impression and then ends up coming across as inauthentic. Some teachers act deceptively inside the yoga studio to live up to the yogin image they have created but have a completely different personality outside the studio. Another limitation in a not-so-exemplary teacher is neglecting to listen to or understand their students.

The Successful Yoga Teacher

Everyone has a different definition of success. For our purposes here, I would define a successful yoga teacher as one who is bringing in a consistent and healthy income, is teaching the kind of students they enjoy working with, and has their desired schedule of private lessons and a well-attended schedule of group classes. A successful teacher may also be well known and respected in their community.

I see success as stemming from two different categories of personal qualities: those that are deep and reflective, and those that are superficial.

Deep Aspects of Successful Teachers

Deep aspects of success arise from conscious thought about what kind of success we want. One teacher's definition of success may be quite different from that of other teachers or of the yoga world at large.

A teacher who is successful on their own terms takes into account how much money they wish and need to make and how many students and what types of student they want to work with. They know their core values and why they have made these choices. Their thinking about these questions helps them formulate a clear mission statement (which we'll discuss on pages 39–40). In addition to knowing what kind of success you want, to be successful you'll also have to take actions and develop habits to make your vision into a reality. Overall, success requires goals, vision, and discipline.

BEING TRUE TO YOURSELF

As yoga has become more popular, trends and fads have proliferated — hot flow, yoga with themed and DJ'd music, glow-in-the-dark yoga, and so forth. It's not unusual to see hybrid offerings that combine yoga and wine tasting, yoga and chocolate, or yoga and pole dancing! Once you have defined your values and goals, you may choose to explore this sort of innovation in your teaching. And if you prefer to maintain a more traditional path, you can do so gracefully and professionally, without feeling threatened and without condemning or mocking those who do otherwise.

Superficial Qualities of Successful Teachers

There are certain other qualities that may contribute to success that I call superficial because we don't have to dig deep to attain them: we were born with them or came by them earlier in life. Some of these qualities include a certain mystique, something about an instructor's personality that seems to create an atmosphere in the classroom that makes students want to come back.

- *Beauty:* A teacher who is attractive or good-looking by society's standards, or a former model or actor trained in effective self-presentation, may have a greater chance of success. Of course we hope this teacher is also skilled and exemplary, but sadly, in this world people often choose eye candy over competence and character.
- *Connections:* Any teacher who has good professional connections to begin with will naturally have a career advantage.
- *Timing:* Being in the right place at the right time can help. As I mentioned earlier, I became a teacher shortly before yoga exploded in popularity in the United States. Riding that wave placed me in a good spot for a successful career, so I feel very lucky.
- *Financial security:* You've probably met a teacher who manages their money well or has money in the bank already. Sometimes people like this succeed as teachers simply because they are not nervous or uptight about finances and have greater access to training, clothing, and resources that enhance their career.
- *Innate physical prowess:* Instagram features endless pictures of naturally bendy yogins — often former gymnasts, acrobats, athletes, or martial artists — who have built huge social media followings because of their physical capability. Whether they were born exceptionally flexible and strong or worked hard to get that way, having a bendy, advanced asana practice can be a source of inspiration to students and increase one's chances of success.
- *Gender:* Although this might sound cynical, being a male yoga teacher in a mostly woman-dominated market has its advantages. While there are millions of successful

and popular women yoga teachers, men can sometimes be more popular at the studio simply because they are something of a novelty.

- *Fashion sense:* A distinct and clear personal style or fashion sense can be an advantage, enhancing a teacher's most attractive features and making them stand out in the crowd.

- *Marketing acumen:* While marketing and social networking skills can be cultivated and learned, some people just have a knack for technology and a natural affinity for marketing and promotion. Using social media comes easily to these people. Of course, many successful yogins eschew technology, preferring to base their teaching and their business on face-to-face personal relationships. The fact remains, however, that many yogins who are adept at social media and marketing are building monumental followings that help their classes fill more quickly, land endorsement deals, and garner paid partnerships in exchange for shout-outs. (In fact, some yogins are earning more through social media than through teaching!)

- *Compelling background:* Some yoga teachers have survivor stories, meaning that they survived something tragic or difficult in life that people relate to. Students will often seek help with a similar challenge in their own lives by studying with such a teacher. I don't wish any kind of survivor story on anyone, but for teachers who are willing to share the wisdom gained from such an experience, it can help draw students.

- *Yoga pedigree:* Some students seek out yoga teachers who have studied directly under legendary teachers like B.K.S. Iyengar, Pattabhi Jois, or their disciples. Because a connection to a very well-known yoga teacher can increase your own visibility, training and apprenticing with such a teacher is not only effective for your education but also potentially helpful for your career later on.

Identifying Areas of Potential Improvement

In reviewing these definitions of skilled, exemplary, and successful teachers, you've probably recognized aspects of yourself and areas where you excel. I hope you also contemplate changes and improvements you'd like to make in your practice, teaching, and career and the goals you want to pursue. The easiest way to start improving is to highlight some of the qualities listed above that you could enhance, and then take action to fill in the gaps.

For example, to become more skilled, would you benefit from training with a different teacher or at a more advanced level? Could you video-record your class so that you can watch yourself and look for ways to refine your teaching?

To work toward becoming exemplary, could you be more honest with your students about the fact that you actually do enjoy a glass of wine on occasion, or could you work on building more community and encouraging conversation with students by inviting them on a group outing after class?

To consider ways you might become more successful, let's do a more detailed self-assessment and look at how to define your core values, which are the basis of your mission statement and the choices and goals you make for yourself and your career.

Discovering Your Core Values

Successful companies orient themselves around a clear set of core values. So can yoga teachers! Core values are the fundamental beliefs or principles that drive your actions. They are what makes you tick and what truly inspires you. To get your set of core values clear, you must be able to explore — with ruthless honesty — what matters most in your life.

Knowing your core values helps define who you are as a person and as a professional. These values consciously and unconsciously drive your decision making in every aspect of your life. If you orient your life around your core values, there is no need to push yourself to be motivated or to spend too long agonizing over decisions: your values will motivate and guide you. In addition, connecting to your core values will help you:

- be more passionate about your teaching
- be more authentic
- build your student base and find colleagues and partners who share your values
- be clear about your future path and make strategic decisions for your career
- stay focused on what matters most in your life and career

Determining what your core values are is fairly easy; living by them, however, takes courage. Among other things, it means being willing to say no to opportunities that don't align with your values. For example, if you don't agree with the values of a studio where you've been offered work, living by your core values will mean turning down the offer — and the potential income.

Sticking to your values also means being able to withstand criticism. Some people will share and endorse your values, and others will find them unattractive. If your values are obviously pushing lots of other people's buttons, you might want to reconsider your reasoning or your self-presentation. However, even if your values are authentic and truly yours (and not those you've passively absorbed from others), and you are striving to live by them, you will likely encounter at least a little disagreement. But I've found that stirring up a bit of controversy isn't a bad thing. One example is a video made by our team at 90 Monkeys in response to the "Shit Girls Say" video that went viral. Our variation on the theme, "Shit Unprofessional Yoga Teachers Say," was definitely controversial, but it has received more than 127,000 views and brought a lot of traffic to our site.

If you have the courage, living by your core values will distinguish you as a leader and a teacher. Your bravery will be rewarded by energy and passion in your yoga career.

COMMON CORE VALUES

Here are some examples of our graduates' values:

Responsibility	Having an impact
Leadership	Uplifting
Respect	Service
Community	Design sense
Integrity	Ingenuity
Generosity	Setting standards
Space	Nurturing
Creativity	Support
Grace	Quest
Dignity	Excellence
Educating others	Mastery
Having fun	

There are a number of ways to come up with your list of core values. Five is a good number to aim for. One way is to talk to the people closest to you. These should be people who know you well and who you trust to be honest with you. Run a few words or phrases by them and get their feedback. For example, you may think of authenticity and generosity as two of your core values. Other people can let you know if your actions are typically in line with those concepts and whether you "walk your talk."

You can also try this exercise in reverse, inferring your values from your actions rather than checking to see if your actions match your stated ideals. Think of two or three choices or decisions you've made recently. Look at the action you ultimately took and think about what values it reveals. For example, if you passed up a promotion that would have entailed moving across the country, you may have been influenced by your spouse's career, your children's education, or the needs of your aging parents. What values does this choice reveal? If, instead, you chose to take the job, what values did that decision reflect?

Another exercise that I found very helpful comes from a seminar with success coaches Jim Bunch and Jack Canfield. Describe the following scenarios to a trusted friend or mentor, and have them jot down key words you use while you tell your stories. Don't overthink what you are saying, and keep each story to about two minutes.

1. Consider a time in your life when everything was going well for you, a time that you look back at and say, "That was the best time of my life!"
2. Consider a time in your life when you were devastated and nothing was going well for you.

Ask your friend to tally how many times you repeat the same words or concepts as you tell the two stories. In the second part of the exercise, some of the words you use will be negative, the opposites of your values. For example, if you repeat a phrase like "I felt like I was alone and had no friends," it probably reflects that one of your core values is community and friendship. The words you've used the most are bound to reflect your core values.

You can also contemplate your values by yourself, writing down your thoughts, or look at the ways other people have approached this question. In his *Autobiography*, Benjamin Franklin listed thirteen virtues he aspired to live by. They're listed on the website ThirteenVirtues.com.

Understanding Why You Teach

The mission statement is a succinct, one- or two-sentence statement about the nature and purpose of your business. Before you try to write yours, I encourage you to think deeply about specifically why you teach yoga. (You may find it interesting to jot down an answer now, and then another after answering the questions below.)

After writing my own mission statement as a yoga teacher, I discovered that on days when I was not inspired to teach, if I simply recalled my highest reason for teaching, I could instantly think of a focus for the class or a theme I wanted to share. I'd get energized and look forward to seeing who'd be in the studio, and I was much more eager to motivate my students to express themselves in their poses.

Why do you teach yoga? Ask yourself the following questions:

- Why does your yoga business exist?
- How does it benefit people?
- If you were not teaching yoga, what would the world miss out on?
- What skills were you born with?

- What are your unique talents?
- What do you feel you were born to do on this planet?
- Why do you personally love to teach yoga?

SOME ANSWERS FROM OUR TRAINEES

- **If you were not teaching yoga, what would the world miss out on?**

  Kindness

  Community

  Self-love

  Empowerment

  Inspiration

  Self-acceptance

  Reflection

  Healing

  Possibility

  Self-connection

  Fun

  Playfulness

  A way to tune back in to the body and intuition

  An opportunity to be happy about who we are

- **What are your unique talents?**

  Humor

  Bringing people together

  Building community

  Communicating

  Using themes and metaphors (taking it "off the mat")

  Functional anatomy

  Reminding others that they can shine

- **Why do you personally love to teach yoga?**

  Seva (service)

  Sharing my gifts

  Getting people to smile

  Yoga changed my life for the better, and I want to share that change

  I want to inspire people

> To make the world a better place
> Yoga gave me peace, and I want to give that to
> others
> I get high from seeing people come back to
> themselves

Some people find it hard to compile a list of their talents, especially because some yoga teaching trains us to be humble and to suppress the ego. But not sharing your gifts can be a disservice to the community. And you have to recognize and value your gifts in order to know you have something vital to share. Your relationship with the ego is healthy when you remember the source of your power — the divine. (By contrast, if you think you deserve sole credit for all your skills and talents, then yes, your ego may be a problem.) The more you understand and own the gifts you were born with, the sooner you can start making a difference in this world!

Your Mission Statement

It's time to put your self-reflection and analysis into the form of a concise mission statement. This doesn't have to follow the format of statements found in a traditional business plan. (However, a formal business plan can help you solidify your plan and business, and you will likely need one if you are applying for loans or seeking financial backing for a teaching business.) I think of the mission statement more as a way for us to ground our teaching goals. We know what we are about, and if asked, we can explain our mission clearly to others.

What should a statement look like? It should convey who

you are, what you do, what you stand for, and why you do it. It can indicate what kind of people you are serving and what benefits you offer them. Your mission statement should explain why your teaching business exists.

Consider the factors you've identified so far — your teaching strengths and areas of potential improvement, your core values, your reasons for teaching — and write your mission statement with them in mind. This is your chance to envision a world that is transformed through your teaching, a world that benefits from your greatest passions and natural talents. Have fun with it. Give yourself plenty of time to refine your statement, and run it by friends and people who have been influential in your life.

Here is my latest mission statement:

My mission is to inspire people to experience their interconnection with all of life while reaching their potential in many dimensions: personal, professional, emotional, and spiritual. Through leadership, writing, and teaching, I'm here to help others become more conscious and awake, living as sustainable stewards of the earth who care deeply about our collective humanity — all while having an adventurously good time.

If you are new to teaching, perhaps this is the first time you've tried to put such a statement together. If you are a veteran teacher, you may want to refine a statement you created previously. In any case, it's a good idea to revisit your mission statement every few years, since you are always changing and growing.

Identifying Your Ideal Students and Their Needs

The above exercises are intended to help us understand who we are as teachers, what matters most to us, and what we hope to gain from teaching. But successful teaching — and a successful business — requires two-way interaction. We also need to understand and respect the expectations, abilities, and personal circumstances of our students and teach them in a way that helps them meet their goals. In business terms, we need to identify our market. With so many yoga students out there, we are free to choose which types of students we most enjoy teaching and tailor our business to appeal to them.

In practical terms, what do students want? If you are teaching yoga to a clearly defined group — expectant mothers, back pain sufferers, or cancer survivors — the answer might be obvious. Conversely, among a diverse group, like students at a high-end spa or a local YMCA, we would anticipate a wider range of abilities and expectations.

In general, I have found that students' expectations for a yoga class are often not clearly defined. Beginners want to experience some of the physical, mental, and emotional benefits they have heard about, while more-advanced students often simply want more of the benefits they are already getting from their practice.

As teachers, we need to strike a balance between offering what we think is best for our students (perhaps things they haven't even thought about) and satisfying their expectations.

How do we strike this balance? First and foremost, we listen — and we create an environment that invites conversation, ideally before or after class. Here are some ways to connect with students:

- Take a moment at the start of class to ask not just about a student's familiarity with yoga but also about special concerns.
- Ask students with limitations, injuries, or any other special needs to raise their hands so you can talk to them before class and also check in with them during and afterward.
- Give every brand-new student a questionnaire asking what they hope to gain from yoga and asking them to list any injuries or limitations.

You can't tailor an entire class of twenty students to the particular limitations of one or two, but if you maintain an openness toward students in a mixed-level class, students with special needs will feel comfortable approaching you to discuss them. Make it clear to students that questions are welcome, and encourage them to speak up immediately if anything hurts, so that you can assist the students in their alignment.

In our teacher training workshops, we ask teachers to list what they believe the average yoga student wants out of a yoga class. Here are some of the answers we've received from yoga teachers all over the world:

Kindness
Challenge
To feel good about themselves
To feel better physically and emotionally
Relaxation
Fitness
Flexibility
Connection to community
To feel supported
To move

To feel safe
To improve lives
Time out to relax
Better connection to self
To meet like-minded people
Stress relief
Time for themselves
To restore energy

Yoga Journal's "Yoga in America" study respondents reported the following as the top five reasons for starting and continuing to practice:

1. Flexibility
2. Stress relief/reduction
3. General fitness/conditioning
4. Improvement of overall health
5. Physical fitness

Exploring your mission as a teacher, discovering your core values, and identifying your ideal students and what they need will give you a road map to guide you toward success as a yoga teacher.

Part II

GETTING DOWN TO BUSINESS

CHAPTER THREE

Yoga Business Basics

In the last chapter we addressed the first step to success: defining what you want. The next step is figuring out how to get there. This chapter covers some of the practical aspects of being a yoga teacher: identifying and selecting business channels, building a student base, retaining students, and marketing your skills and talents. If you've been teaching on a full-time basis for a while, some of this will be familiar and you may wish to either use it as a review or skip ahead.

There are many sources of income for yoga teachers, involving different periods, levels, and types of commitment, and drawing on different business skills. For example, organizing a yoga retreat involves not only planning and teaching classes but also marketing, organizing accommodations and meals, accounting, and administration. Private lessons are based on individual relationships, and workshops are focused on content. Being a yoga professional requires us to juggle many balls, swim in many streams, wear many hats — pick your metaphor.

I can quickly think of eleven business channels:

1. Beginner series/classes
2. Specialty series
3. Group classes
4. Private lessons
5. Workshops
6. Teacher trainings
7. Retreats
8. Conferences and festivals
9. Product sales
10. Partnerships and endorsements
11. Teaching in workplaces and at schools, colleges, and continuing education venues

Let's look more closely at these. (And see chapter 4 for a discussion of how the first six of these business channels can be adapted for online teaching.)

Beginner Series/Classes

What did you think about your first yoga teacher? When I asked yoga teachers this question, most of them reported thinking that their first teacher was the best ever! This teacher was a role model who taught them well, gave them something they value greatly, and got them hooked on the practice. Being a student's first yoga teacher is a privilege — and a responsibility, because a bad first experience with a teacher can turn a student off from yoga forever.

From the perspective of a teacher, it can be very rewarding to help beginners, who are first experiencing the gifts of yoga. From a professional perspective, beginner yoga students are a gift to treasure. If you are not reaching out to the beginner population, you are missing a wonderful opportunity.

Students who already do yoga also already have teachers. A bunch of teachers all attempting to teach to the same population of students can work against one another in unnecessary ways. Running a regular beginner series can be a great solution to this problem. Beginner series can be offered monthly, quarterly, or biannually depending on student demand, and each series usually runs for four to eight weeks.

In Boulder, Colorado, where I live, a large percentage of the population practices yoga, and there are also lots of yoga teachers. I've heard many of these teachers complain about the surplus of teachers and the scarcity of students. But even in locations like Boulder, where lots of people do yoga, *there will always be many more who don't (yet)*. Many are curious about yoga and perhaps have a friend who practices. More and more often, doctors are recommending yoga to patients as a way to relieve pain and stress. Athletes have heard it's good for their muscles, and elderly students understand that it can help them maintain their mobility. Recruiting new students from among these populations can spare you from friction with other teachers and enables you to form the special bond between the students and you, as their first teacher. Students like these will stick with you for the long haul: from there they can matriculate into group classes, private lessons, workshops, and all your other offerings.

The practical advantage of teaching a beginner series, or any other kind of series, if you charge in advance, is that you can plan on a specific level of income for an extended period. You can also plan a good part of your schedule ahead of time.

To derive the greatest benefit from this business channel, offer these series regularly throughout the year. In addition, make sure there is a basic or mixed-level class for your graduates to attend when they complete the series so they have a way to continue their practice!

Specialty Series

Whether you're an independent yoga teacher or a studio owner/manager, another way to reach students who may not already be practicing yoga regularly, or to appeal to current students, is to offer series of classes tailored to specific groups or needs. Some examples include yoga for the lower back, yoga for cyclists, prenatal yoga, yoga for men, or yoga for runners.

PLAYING TO YOUR STRENGTHS

To come up with ideas for series that would be fun and effective for you to teach, brainstorm by making a list of your strengths and interests and match that to possible series topics. For example, you might be naturally inclined toward helping people with injuries and thus could offer a yoga series such as "Yoga for the Lower Back" or "Yoga for Shoulders." Or perhaps you are a gifted athlete in a particular sport. If so, then you can help those in your sport get more freedom through yoga by leading a series called, for example, "Yoga for Runners."

Group Classes

Group classes are the most common income source for yoga teachers. Perhaps the most rewarding aspect of teaching group classes is the sense of community that builds when a group practices together consistently over time.

When you teach at a studio, you'll either be paid a flat fee for your class or be paid "by the head," or per student. Some studios will pay a combination of both.

Being paid by the head places more of the incentive for marketing the class on the teacher, making it a collaborative effort between the studio and the teacher. A flat fee puts the marketing onus only on the studio. Having both parties marketing the class is a win-win.

The advantage of being paid a flat fee is that you can depend on a steady income no matter how many students attend your class. The downside is that flat fees are typically not very high. When paid a flat fee, although you may not make as much income, think of it as a way to build a loyal base of students who will funnel into your workshops, series, or retreats. And as always, consistently show up for class, give students a challenging but safe practice, and do not sub out your class too often!

Private Lessons

Private classes pay the highest hourly rate (after teacher trainings). Although they can be more taxing, especially if you travel to students' homes, four to seven private lessons a week can provide a good, reliable chunk of weekly income. You might want to set a goal of working with a certain number of private clients per week. The intimacy of teaching private lessons can be too intense for some yoga teachers, though, so you might also choose not to offer them.

To build this business channel, keep track of your students' progress in a notebook or file so you are always sharing fresh teachings and have clear boundaries around time. And don't be afraid to invite a student to take private lessons with you!

Workshops

Workshops often take place on a weekend or over a few consecutive weeknights. They can target many of the interest groups mentioned above: pregnant women, athletes, kids, cancer survivors, men, golfers. There's an almost endless variety of opportunities for niche teaching in addition to general options.

To build this channel, survey your regular students about what kinds of things they want to learn more about in yoga. Pay attention to how students respond to what you teach in your regular classes: what teachings do they seem to love, or what poses do they need more practice with? These observations could spark some desirable workshop themes. Then when the time comes to offer a workshop, students will be hungry for what you have to share.

Teacher Trainings

If you have a knack for teaching others the "science" behind how you teach what you teach, teacher training might be a natural evolution for you once you've been teaching yoga for a while. Teacher training has two facets: teaching people to become new yoga teachers and working with existing yoga teachers to improve their teaching skills.

Training other teachers is definitely not for everyone; in fact, there are veteran yoga teachers who are wildly popular but who have rarely, if ever, trained other teachers. It's just not their thing. If teacher training is for you, you'll probably know: you'll feel a natural pull to help others in this capacity, and you might be invited to be part of the faculty for a teacher training. Being invited is always a good sign that others believe in your talents and want what you have to offer.

Teacher training as a business channel pays very well, since professional training tuitions command a higher price than group classes or workshops. Tuition can be higher because it represents an investment for trainees and offers a certification toward a career path. And when you've gotten to the point in your career that you have enough knowledge and aptitude to teach other teachers, your expertise is worthy of higher compensation.

There are two teacher training business models. First, you can run and administrate your own training independently. In this scenario you handle all revenue and pay yourself accordingly after expenses.

Alternatively, you might be on faculty through a studio or other organization, which is more typical for newer teachers. In this case, you are less involved in the marketing of the training, and there are a couple of ways you can be compensated. The first way is to set an hourly rate for your time. Typically this is twice what you would charge hourly for private lessons. The second compensation option is based on the projected revenue from the training program and the number of students who enroll. For trainings hosted by a third-party studio, the typical arrangement is to split the net profits 60:40 or 70:30 in favor of the teacher. If you teach only part of the training, you can ask to be paid a fee proportional to the part you teach. For example, if you teach 5 hours of a 180-hour training, that represents 2.7 percent (5÷180) of the total hours. Calculate this percentage of the net profit and then split it 70:30 with the studio.

In order to cultivate teacher training as a business

channel, listen to your intuition as to whether teacher training is for you. If it is, prepare well, and be very realistic about
managing students' expectations. Students invest a lot more
in teacher training than other programs, so rather than prom-
ising all kinds of perks and outcomes and then underdeliver-
ing because the demands of the training were too much for
you to handle, promise "low" and then overdeliver.

Retreats

Retreats are a fantastic way to build community, take your
students deeper into the practice, and get away to an exotic
location. They involve a great deal of work before, during, and
after — but, hey, you get to spend time in a beautiful spot
and maybe tack on a vacation if you can spare the time! Because of the planning required and the expenses of renting
a facility, retreats are not always financially lucrative, but the
finances can work out well if you have a large number of students who want to travel with you. When your students have a
good time, they are more likely to become long-term clients,
so despite the hard work retreats require, they can be a reasonable investment in your community and career.

To excel with retreats, think about hiring an assistant to
help you oversee the retreat administration and ensure that
your students are well taken care of. Like a teacher training
program, a retreat is a high-ticket item for participants, so
make sure you manage expectations well.

Conferences and Festivals

Teaching at events such as conferences and festivals will
give you good visibility and potentially attract new students.

However, to be invited to teach at such an event, you need a fairly well-established reputation and a loyal student base. Again, because of the preparation time, travel, and teaching time involved, the financial reward may not be all that high.

If you're serious about building this business channel, be prompt in all your dealings and emails with festival organizers and stay on top of marketing tasks. Answering emails and providing workshop descriptions in a timely manner go a long way. Yoga teachers who are unresponsive do not get asked back.

Product Sales

The market for yoga products such as instructional materials, props, clothing, bags, and other accessories is huge. You can benefit by creating your own yoga product or selling someone else's product on your website or in person. However, selling products during classes can be a sensitive issue, since students have paid money for your teaching and may not be receptive to sales pitches. Furthermore, creating any pressure for students to buy products may represent an abuse of the teacher-student relationship. Whether you are comfortable selling things in or around yoga classes depends on how you feel about yoga and consumerism. My personal take is that yoga cannot shelter us from the fact that we are consumers, any more than we can stop outside noise from happening when we meditate. Therefore, if you are excited to sell cool products to support your students' practices as part of this business channel, go for it — just do it tastefully and tactfully. Choose products you can be comfortable endorsing, sourced from vendors that offer sustainably manufactured yoga products.

Partnerships and Endorsements

With the many competing brands of yoga-related clothing, props, and accessories now available, many companies rely on yoga teachers to promote their products, much like big apparel and equipment brands sponsor athletes. You may already be doing it for free if you've worn an outfit or sported a prop and had one of your students or colleagues approach you and ask, "Where did you get that?" Modeling products is effective marketing.

Many of these sellers will approach yoga teachers who are well regarded in their communities about becoming an "ambassador." Most will ask a teacher to wear or display their merchandise in exchange for free products and mentioning their name in a blog or a social networking post here and there. Such relationships are typically not exclusive: you can still wear and use other brands. If you have a large enough number of social media followers and influence, however, you can sometimes negotiate an exclusive promotional arrangement with a brand, by which you agree to use only their products in your teaching and public appearances in exchange for a fee.

If you're hoping to develop this channel, the key is to be patient. You'll also want to establish yourself as a thought leader in the field, which means writing articles and blogs and building a robust social media following on platforms like Facebook, Instagram, and TikTok.

Teaching in Workplaces and at Schools

Teaching workplace yoga, or "corporate yoga," as it is sometimes called, can be extremely fulfilling. You can make a huge difference in employees' comfort, health, and productivity. For employees who sit hunched over their computers for hours with endless deadlines to meet, you are a breath of fresh air! You can teach a variety of poses to counter the effects of sitting, "computer neck," low back pain, and hunched shoulders that afflict millions of workers, as well as teaching them breathing, meditation, and other mindfulness techniques to help boost their productivity and consciousness.

Corporate yoga instruction can be set up in two ways. First, it can be arranged through a wellness agent in your area who acts as a sort of broker, connecting companies with wellness experts and fitness trainers. If you can find such a broker or business, you can drop off your résumé or offer them complimentary classes so that they can see how you teach. If you're a fit, they can start placing you with companies looking to bring yoga into their facilities.

When I first started teaching, I was lucky enough to have such an agent come to a class at the studio where I taught. After taking my class, she brought me on board immediately, and from there I went on to teach executives at Atlantic Records, Bear Stearns, and Pfizer. I am still in touch with some of the students I taught, and some even went on to become yoga teachers!

The second way to arrange corporate yoga classes is to set up the program yourself directly with the company. For me, this happened organically when students attending my group classes approached me about teaching in their workplace. One of the coolest programs I organized was teaching the cast and crew of the Broadway show *Beauty and the Beast*. "The Beast" was a regular in my group classes and asked me to come to the theater to teach!

Many companies are looking for relatively low-cost ways to offer employee benefits and decrease health-care costs, and yoga classes are appealing on both counts. The best way to approach a company is through its human resources department, whose staff can get the word out to employees.

When you are arranging a corporate program, you'll want to ask who is paying: will the employees be covering the classes, or is the company willing to offer the classes to employees as a perk? Or perhaps the company is willing to pay for half of the class fee while the employee covers the rest.

The most straightforward option is for the company to cover the entire cost and compensate you directly. In this case, you should charge what you would for teaching a private class in a client's home, plus 10 to 20 percent to cover multiple students. However, not all businesses can afford to offer their employees free yoga classes. Either way, it's best if the human resources department handles your payment. If the employees pay part of the class fee, the company can determine what to charge, based on your flat fee, and collect the fee from them.

There are other ways to handle pricing and compensation, such as being paid by the head, but the above methods require the least amount of administrative work on your part.

Teaching yoga in schools or other educational venues requires networking. Again, students in your regular group classes might approach you about opportunities to lead yoga classes in their club, school, or gym. If you are a parent, you might talk with the teachers at your children's school about offering yoga. You can follow the same approach to pricing and compensation that we recommend above for corporate yoga, keeping in mind that budgets may not be as high as in corporate settings.

Doing the Numbers

When you're deciding how and how much you want to teach, it's helpful to sit down and think hard about your personal and financial situation. First, look at how much money you *need* to live and pay your expenses. Then consider how much income you *want* in order to be, do, and have everything you value in life. This, of course, brings up the question of whether a yoga teacher's income can ever really cover all that we want to be, do, and have. My answer is that yoga may never fulfill our wildest financial dreams, but it can provide a decent annual income with the freedom to create your own schedule and work on your own terms. And if it doesn't meet your financial needs or desires completely, you may have to supplement it with a day job and/or pursue other ways of earning part of your living. The key is to maximize what you can earn, and that takes foresight and planning.

As a professional, you want to look at the different channels available to you, assess which ones are your strongest and weakest sources of income, and then determine whether you'd like to add a new channel or improve a channel that could be more lucrative.

If you are interested in adding a new business channel, a first step is to visualize yourself succeeding at it. You can add it as a symbol on your altar or *puja* where you meditate, even if it is just a phrase on a sticky note like "I am leading a beautiful retreat in Mexico." Next, take action toward augmenting the channels that interest you most. For example, take a course on how to offer a retreat, go on a retreat yourself, or attend a variety of workshop events to see what it would be like. Ask for help from other teachers who have done it before.

When refining business channels you already have in

place, examine how well you are managing all aspects of that source of income. Are your classes consistently well attended? If not, consider what you might change. Are they offered at appealing times? Do people know about the classes? Are they enthusiastically promoted, and is that promotion targeted in savvy ways? Think about the quality of your teaching. If we're honest, most of us know if we routinely fall short in some way.

Once you have determined which business channels you want to focus on, start making specific plans, such as how many times a year you want to offer programs like specialty series, retreats, and workshops. Balance these with your regular weekly commitments, like group classes and private lessons.

Last, map out these offerings on your yearly calendar and then create a marketing plan (see pages 132–34) to ensure that each event and ongoing offering is a success. Whether you plan to implement these offerings immediately or are planning for the future, you can map out the entire year and estimate an annual income that accommodates your needs and wants.

Creating a Balanced Teaching Schedule

If you are a new teacher, it's best to refine your teaching by focusing on your group classes. You might also start working to build your private clientele and plan ahead for offering a beginner series in your area.

A nicely balanced schedule at this point might look something like this:

Ongoing Offerings

- *Private lessons:* Four lessons per week
- *Group classes:* Eight to fifteen classes per week

Beginner Series

- Monthly or every other month

As you advance, you become ready to start leading workshops, retreats, or specialty series. I knew I was ready to handle these extra offerings when two things started to happen:

1. My students asked me to lead more in-depth workshops and started requesting that I take them on retreat to an exotic locale.
2. Studio owners invited me to teach a workshop, and I was invited to colead a teacher training.

As I mentioned earlier, when people begin to invite you to do things, it's probably a sign that you're ready and the demand is there. Although it is possible to start offering workshops or retreats before being asked, I can guarantee that offerings will be more successful, and you will feel more confident and well received, if someone else has invited you first. From a marketing perspective, if someone invites you, they will actively support your efforts. If you invite yourself, they may have less enthusiasm because it was your idea, not theirs.

REMEMBER YOUR OWN ONGOING EDUCATION

As you plan your teaching offerings, it's important to allow time and resources for your own ongoing education. I like to include some form of continuing education for myself at least once a quarter, whether that is an in-person event or some kind of online learning. The kind of program you choose is up to you; it needs to fit your budget and your personal and teaching obligations. Online learning is usually less expensive and more convenient than traveling somewhere to take a class. However, nothing can replace the experience of being in the same room with other students and a teacher who can observe you in person. Either way, I recommend budgeting 5 to 10 percent of your income for continuing education! Prioritize this kind of savings commitment for education, even when it seems impossible: it is vital for keeping you fresh and inspired and ultimately boosting your business.

If you are a seasoned teacher who is ready to teach or already teaching workshops, retreats, and specialty series, continually add events to your schedule. Also, you might teach fewer ongoing group classes and devote more time to other, more financially rewarding offerings. You might set up a target schedule like the following:

Specialty Series/Classes and Retreats

Beginner series: Four to six per year (seasonal)
Workshops: Four per year (seasonal)
Full retreat: One or more weeklong getaways to exotic locales
     per year
Long-weekend retreats: One or two seasonal mini-getaways
     per year
Specialty series: Two to four per year
Fundraiser benefit classes: One to three per year

Ongoing Offerings

- *Private lessons:* Four to six lessons per week
- *Group classes:* Six to ten classes per week

GIFT CERTIFICATES

One way to promote offerings such as private lessons, beginner series, and specialty series is to offer holiday or special-occasion gift certificates. The December holidays are a great opportunity!

Five Steps to Building a Solid Student Base

As part of yoga business basics, I advise my clients to think about how to develop a strong student base. I have boiled it down to a five-step process through which teachers reach students and inspire them to come to class, stay with the practice, and become loyal to the practice — and to you, as their teacher.

The five steps may not sound "yoga-like." That's because we borrowed them from corporate/business terminology. We use them because it's helpful to have language to describe this process, but we do not mean to cheapen the experience or to commodify students! The results of applying this five-step process go back to our highest vision: more people doing yoga to help build a more conscious world.

1. Identify and Reach

The first step in the process is to identify the types of students you want to teach. You might think of them according to occupation: office workers, schoolteachers, nurses, military personnel, or stay-at-home parents. Or you might think about categories of needs: new moms, athletes, children, people with chronic pain, people in recovery, or people with depression or anxiety. You can probably identify many more categories.

To reach a group of potential students, you must consider

what that group most wants. Can you provide it? This is the *value proposition*.

For example, if you are reaching out to parents with new babies, what would be the value of yoga to a new mother or father? Possibilities include:

Time for themselves
Rehabilitating the body after pregnancy
Better sleep
Cultivating patience
Cultivating gentleness
Accepting imperfection
Encouraging body acceptance
Companionship with other new parents
Confidence to step into a new life
Community

Once you've identified your target group, think about how you could reach out to them. For new parents, possible points of contact include:

Pediatric offices
Midwives/doulas
Baby stores
Breastfeeding groups
Parent support groups
Mom-and-baby groups
Kindergartens
Day care centers
Playgroups and other children's activities
Schools
Social networking groups
Coffee shops

Now, let's look at how to serve a much different population: athletes. You might reason that they want:

Better performance in a sport
Cross-training
Improved balance
Injury prevention and recovery
Increased body awareness
Flexibility
Improved focus
Enhanced recovery from training
Pain relief

Places where you could reach this group include:

Workplaces
Physical therapy offices
Running groups
Cycling groups
Facebook groups
Orthopedic offices
Health clubs
Sporting events (races, games, competitions)
Sporting goods retailers

For these two groups, both the value propositions and
the possible points of contact are dramatically different (even
though some individuals might fit in both categories!). This
difference illustrates how much skill and awareness is involved in reaching new clients.

When you've identified the value proposition that aligns
most closely with your students' needs, your programming becomes much more effective. Now you can convey that value
proposition clearly in your promotional materials, in social

media posts, and in person when you announce your events and programs. You'll be able to qualify the benefits of your offering in such a way that students will want to say yes to signing up. When you're teaching, you can target your yoga classes so that they're specifically geared toward your students' needs and desires.

2. Acquire

Acquiring a student refers to the moment when someone signs up for one of your classes. The exact acquisition process will depend on where you are teaching. It may require the student to register at the facility, sign up for specific classes, complete waivers or questionnaires and health forms, and arrange payment. If you are an independent teacher working at a studio, the studio may handle most of this process.

The acquisition period often forms the first (and most lasting) impression for students; it's imperative to make sure they are welcomed and given a proper orientation to the facility and the class. For example, it is customary to show new students where they can change and leave their belongings, where the bathrooms are, and how to get props and a towel if they need them. This can be an overwhelming time for a new student and frequently for the teacher as well. The student may be completely unfamiliar with yoga and feel intimidated in a new environment. The teacher may be inundated with questions from new students while trying to prepare for class. This is a key moment to model remaining poised, calm, inviting, and reassuring.

During the Acquire phase (and actually during all phases), it is imperative to respond to prospective students in a timely manner. When you get back to students quickly, it leaves a very good impression and you will be more likely to see positive results in registrations and sales. It seems the busier those in customer care become, the rarer it is to find businesses whose response time is swift. Being responsive and timely will help you stand out in the crowd.

3. Teach

Do your absolute best to engage new students through being prepared and present in your teaching. Draw on all the qualities discussed in chapter 2 that make you a skilled and exemplary teacher.

Teach in a creative, innovative, and dynamic way that makes students want to return. You want your students to get great results. Constantly hone your craft by staying current in your own yoga studies and education.

4. Retain

You know you have good overall retention when your class has a core of regular students. The reason they keep coming every week is that your class has become an integral part of their lives and schedules. You want that core group to grow.

What fosters retention? Outstanding teaching is most important, but other small things can go a long way. These include addressing students by name, giving hands-on assists, building relationships outside class, and not subbing out your class too often.

5. Build Loyalty

Loyalty is related to retention, but it's more personal: it means the student would choose your class or studio, even

over other teachers' offerings at more convenient times or locations, because they feel they have received so much from
you. A connection with a loyal student may be lifelong; it's a
relationship almost like what you have with family. It comes
from deep bonding experiences through yoga. I have shared
some heartfelt moments and adventures with students on retreat that connect us for life.

Here are some ways to build loyalty:

- Text students if you haven't seen them for a while, tell
  them you've missed them, and ask if they are okay.
- Invite students to community events like movie nights,
  potlucks, and holiday celebrations.
- Remember to ask clients about their lives rather than
  talking about your own.
- Remember and celebrate birthdays.
- Recognize students' achievements inside and outside
  the classroom.

Understanding these five steps to building a student base
should give you a good overview of a client's journey from
finding you to enjoying your teaching to becoming a long-
term, devoted student. To encourage students to be a part of
your yoga community for years to come, the key is to be aware
of where your students are in this cycle and to continually
follow the approaches suggested above.

CHAPTER FOUR

Online Yoga Business Basics

Online yoga or digital yoga consists of yoga education ("content") taught via the internet, on video conferencing tools such as Zoom or on applications (apps), rather than in person.

As an individual yoga teacher, you can participate in many different formats of online yoga (which I'll get into a little later) either as a hired wellness expert working for a company that is producing online content or by producing your own digital content and handling all aspects of production. This chapter will cover the various business channels and class formats for teaching yoga online, as well as the nuts and bolts of equipment, setup, and preparation. Chapter 12 will give guidance on how to skillfully teach yoga online and how to translate your teaching skills to the online space. But first, some background...

As with many businesses and schools, yoga education started popping up online around 2008. We at Vesselify (formerly 90 Monkeys) were early adopters of online courses, offering professional development training for yoga teachers starting in 2011, and in 2012 I began teaching on-demand application-based yoga classes through YogaGlo (now Glo).

Up until the pandemic began in 2020, most yoga teachers did not have much in the way of digital offerings, teaching primarily in person in local studios or their homes. Those who did already have experience with digital yoga had a knack for film production and content creation via educational courses or platforms like YouTube or Patreon, or they had been recruited by one of the larger digital yoga platforms like Yoga International, Wanderlust, Yoga Journal, Glo, or Alo.

Then in March of 2020 all of that changed. Instantly the digital yoga industry accelerated, and the landscape will never be the same.

As the world locked down to cope with the first wave of Covid-19, in-person yoga classes immediately evaporated. Yoga studios and individual yoga teachers all over the world pivoted quickly to become livestream and film production experts out of their homes in a determined attempt to keep the yoga going (and continue making ends meet financially).

Many studios and yoga teachers did not persevere through the two-plus years of social distancing. So many studios had to close. And many yoga teachers transitioned out of their teaching careers, got different jobs, or pursued other interests. Those who remained grappled with the changed landscape of yoga.

The Pros and Cons of the New Online Yoga

Change is hard to embrace, but embrace it we must. To do so, it can help to look at the positive aspects of how the pandemic changed yoga. Here are some of the observations our community of 300-hour teacher training students made:

- *Increased interest:* At first, those lucky enough to gain time at home became more interested in yoga — and not just asana. Demand increased for some of the less physically oriented aspects of the practice, such as meditation, restorative yoga, Yoga Nidra, philosophy lectures, and pranayama. In our experience, these subjects used to attract mostly yoga teachers, so it was a refreshing change to see nonteachers wanting to fully embrace the practice of yoga instead of considering it just another workout.
- *Ability to study with teachers all over the world:* Yoga enthusiasts delighted in being able to study with their preferred teacher(s) across oceans and time zones, for a fraction of the cost of what it had previously taken to leave home, fly or drive, miss work, and pay for accommodations to attend trainings or retreats.
- *Scheduling flexibility:* Busy people realized they could much more easily fit in short-format yoga practices available online, freeing them from the time commitment required of a sixty- or seventy-five-minute class in the studio, plus the time it took to travel to the studio and back.
- *Unparalleled convenience:* Those who turned to online yoga during quarantine came to love the convenience of online yoga — not only the shorter duration but also the anonymity, not having to deal with transportation, and the ability to do yoga in their PJs at any time of day. I spoke to one busy CEO and dad who, thanks to the pandemic, now does yoga on demand daily at 5:00 AM for thirty minutes just before his

children wake up. Prior, he couldn't maintain a consistent practice at a studio.

As you can see, many yoga enthusiasts got a taste of online yoga because of the pandemic, and they don't want to stop!

While stay-at-home orders initially increased online class attendance dramatically, attrition for online yoga set in toward the beginning of 2022. Digital fatigue is a thing. It's real, and once the pandemic restrictions finally lifted, many yogins were craving in-person experiences again, whether at a yoga studio or, if they could afford it, a yoga retreat. This makes sense, as yoga has traditionally thrived as an in-person modality. It will always be paramount that there be *darshan*, Sanskrit for "to see and be seen." Nothing can replace the three-dimensional setting in which the teacher can observe the students in community and the students in turn can see the teacher.

Despite the trend back toward in-person practice and how fatigued with screens some might be, a large cohort of students who embraced online yoga for the reasons listed above are not going back — especially those who don't have a local teacher or studio nearby. Indeed, *online yoga is not going anywhere anytime soon.*

Now we'll look at the many facets of teaching yoga online from a business and teaching perspective.

Online Terminology

Let's go over some common terminology for online business so we're speaking the same language. Here are some words that get thrown around a lot in the online space and their definitions.

- *Livestream:* Content that is broadcast online live as it is happening. A yoga teacher offers a live broadcast of a class, and students tune in from wherever they are in the world on their personal device.
- *Hybrid:* Classes in which the teacher has students physically in the studio with them and simultaneously livestreams to people at home via a web camera.
- *On demand:* Prerecorded educational videos hosted on a website for viewing either through purchase or as part of a subscription. For example, teachers prerecord their classes (just them and the camera) and then post them online. On demand is a great way to showcase classes with a variety of shorter durations — even as little as five minutes. Livestream and hybrid classes can also be recorded and then offered on demand.
- *Meeting:* An online video meeting can be used for any gathering of multiple participants, but it can also be used for a yoga class or workshop in which a trainer or trainers present live on camera to an audience that can appear on video and be heard on audio. Participants can also interact by typing text into a chat, responding to polls, raising their virtual hands, or unmuting themselves to speak.
- *Webinar:* An online seminar or workshop in which a trainer or trainers present live on camera to an audience that may or may not be able to interact with them. If given access, participants can interact by typing text into a chat, responding to polls, raising their virtual hands, and even asking questions on video. Participants are generally not on camera or audio unless

they are promoted to panelist. Presenters must pay extra for webinar service (vs. regular meeting-hosting capabilities). In the context of yoga instruction, webinar classes are typically used by teachers who draw a big crowd (one hundred or more students at a time).

- *Online courses or e-courses:* Online learning through either on-demand videos combined with livestream classes and their recordings or solely on-demand videos.
- *Asynchronous:* Teachings that do not require live interaction. Learning takes place according to the students' pace. Engagement and efficacy are determined by deadlines and a required competency component such as a quiz.
- *Synchronous:* Teachings that require live interaction with either a trainer or other students. Engagement and efficacy are determined by demonstrating engagement and integration of content. In the context of an online teacher training, synchronous learning would include practice teaching, the lead trainer interacting one-on-one or with a group of students, the use of digital "breakout" rooms (sessions that are split off from the main meeting room that allow participants to meet in smaller groups), and discussion boards.
- *Self-paced learning:* The type of asynchronous instruction that allows the student to control the flow of the coursework.
- *Hybrid or blended learning:* An instructional approach to online courses or trainings that includes a combination of online and in-person learning. For example, students can complete online self-paced assignments

by a certain date and then meet in person or online
for additional learning activities.

• *Learning management software (LMS):* Platforms on
which online learning content is hosted. For example, when you purchase an online course, a link is
provided that takes you to the "hub," where you can
find all the educational videos, PDF downloads, and
other course materials; that hub is the LMS. Examples include Teachable, Kajabi, Thinkific, and Kartra,
to name a few.

How to Earn a Living Teaching Online Yoga

There are several ways to generate income in the online space.
The following is a list of online yoga business channels along
with useful information on what they are and how to optimize each one.

One benefit of most of these models is that you likely
don't have to travel very far, since your teaching, for the most
part, can be operated from home or your local studio with
the right equipment. With that said, you are going to be a
producer and as such will need to invest in production equipment (more on this soon), as well as understand the technology and administration efforts necessary to deliver online
content. Also, you must feel comfortable teaching in front of
the camera. If you tend to clam up or freeze when the camera
is rolling, this is not a good fit for you, or you might need
more time to become more comfortable.

Subscription Model

A subscription business is a recurring revenue model in
which yoga students pay a monthly or yearly fee in exchange

for your yoga classes and other educational content. Students can generally cancel their subscription at any time, effective at the end of the current billing cycle.

BENEFITS

- This model allows you to leverage your student relationships to build a steady stream of passive income.
- It allows students from all over the world to find and work with you.
- You can offer a vast library of classes and teachings with a variety of durations, themes, and goals.

KEEP IN MIND

- The subscription space has become very crowded since the pandemic hit in 2020, when many teachers and studios were forced to transition to online teaching. It can be harder to stand out and challenging to find new subscribers if you're just starting this model.
- You need to be disciplined about filming and posting regular and consistent content. It's important to maintain a good supply of content to keep subscribers engaged and coming back for fresh offerings.

HOW TO INTEGRATE THE SUBSCRIPTION MODEL INTO YOUR REPERTOIRE

There are countless ways to start your own subscription model. You'll need the following components

- An all-in-one membership-hosting service for content creators that includes:

    o   An e-commerce system that can bill students on a

> > recurring basis with a credit card on file (usually monthly or annually)
> > o A website that allows you to host videos and organize them visually
> > o A mechanism to capture subscribers by giving them an initial free trial or a sample class

> Alternatively, you could cobble together these three services yourself, but that tends to be more time-consuming and prone to synchronization issues. Popular membership site-hosting services include Teachable, Union.Fit, OfferingTree, Wix, Namastream, Member-Vault, and Patreon.

- Appropriate class titles, high-quality cover images, and concise, well-written, accurate class descriptions.

Online Drop-In Classes and Workshops

You may choose to teach independently of a yoga studio and market your own drop-in classes or workshops to your audience. They can be offered on demand (prerecorded), as livestreams, or in a hybrid format.

BENEFITS

- Similar to in-person classes, online drop-in classes allow students to attend regular yoga classes whenever it fits their schedule. There is no long-term commitment, and participants can join on a class-by-class basis.
- Students can join you from different time zones, even international locations, and be spontaneous with their decision to join class last-minute.

- Students can book workshops ahead of time or even just a few minutes beforehand without worrying about it selling out (unless you are capping enrollment).
- Similar to in-person workshops, an online workshop is a chance to go more in depth on a topic than is possible in drop-in classes.
- Workshops will bring in revenue in advance of the day you're teaching. Drop-in classes might bring in advance revenue if you sell punch cards or unlimited cards, but otherwise revenue will come as students pay, close to the time of your teaching.

Keep in Mind

- Planning, producing, executing, marketing, and providing customer care for online drop-in classes or workshops require significant administrative effort.
- Because of the continual nature of drop-in classes, it will be necessary to market them on a regular basis, such as by posting a listing of your classes weekly or daily.

How to Integrate Online Drop-In Classes or Workshops into Your Repertoire

To incorporate this model into your teaching, follow these steps:

For drop-in classes:

1. Choose class times for your drop-in classes that suit your schedule and are likely to be convenient for the majority of your student base.
2. Set the pricing for your drop-in classes. Some inde-

pendent teachers price their online classes lower than the going rate for in-person classes; others who have a dedicated student base may choose to match the going rate of studios in their area.

Will you offer à la carte (individual) classes only? A punch card or bundle of multiple classes at a lower rate than individual classes? A monthly unlimited option like those offered by studios? If so, will you have an introductory thirty-day trial offer?

For workshops:

1. Conduct market research by polling your students on topics that interest them for workshops, then select a compelling workshop topic aligned with your community's interests.
2. Set the price of your workshop. Decide if you will have an early price and a regular price or just one.
3. Set up a marketing plan for your workshop (see pages 132–34).

For both drop-in classes and workshops:

1. Implement an e-commerce system to handle payments. Some popular examples of services you can use to get paid include Union.Fit, PayPal, Venmo, Zelle, or Punchpass.
2. Choose a reliable meeting software like Zoom for hosting and recording livestream classes, if applicable.
3. Decide if you want to set up a platform for hosting recorded videos that become part of an online library students can subscribe to.

Online Courses

An online course is an educational program with an organized curriculum or syllabus (typically units or modules) that takes place in a virtual space synchronously, asynchronously, or a combination of both. Online courses can be for personal interest and focused on one skill, such as "How to Improve Your Handstand," or more formal, resulting in specialty certifications or continuing education credits. The duration of an online course depends on the complexity and depth of the subject matter, the course objectives (i.e., whether it is a certification course or continuing education), and its format (synchronous vs. asynchronous, etc.).

Benefits

- Some students find online learning to be more effective than in-person learning, since they can work at their own pace, which leads to more focus.
- Online courses can be recorded and then sold long after you first release them, making them a source of passive income.
- Offering courses on specific, niche subjects establishes you as a subject matter expert in those areas.

Keep in Mind

- On-demand (prerecorded) online courses have a shelf life and, if not carefully planned, can become dated fairly quickly, so you need to be prepared to take them down or refilm them to bring them up to modern standards when needed.
- Planning, producing, executing, marketing, and pro

viding customer care for online courses is time-consuming and can have a steep learning curve; therefore, this channel is not for the faint of heart. Be prepared to work hard before reaping the benefits.

• While the content of your online course may be "evergreen" or timeless, without regular marketing or periods where the course is run with a live component, sales typically stagnate.

How to Integrate Online Courses into Your Repertoire

If you have never created an online course, it can be very helpful to first take an online course on how to make an online course! The essential steps include:

1. Pick a topic you know your audience is interested in learning about — that is, a topic with market interest.
2. Create compelling learning outcomes — that is, clearly define what students will get out of the course.
3. Organize your content into a curriculum — modules and the videos that comprise those modules.
4. Consider whether you want to have a "live cohort" that meets online outside class hours to go over content or to practice skills. These meetups can be for the whole group or smaller groups.
5. Price your course.
6. Decide which content is best filmed in advance (for on demand), and which, if any, will be filmed live with students online and subsequently archived for on demand.
7. Plan for each on-demand video to be about a

single topic, and don't be afraid to plan for short-duration, bite-size videos.

8. Film, record, and edit all content.
9. Set up your online platform — in other words, the website where you will host your course.
10. Launch the course to your network, get the word out, and continually market the course.

As with hosting a subscription site, if you offer à la carte courses, you will want to have a hosting platform that can market and sell your courses. You'll need an e-commerce system that can sell the course and take payments and an LMS that can host the course videos in an organized fashion. Or you can use an all-in-one service that provides both the e-commerce system and LMS. Some such services include Teachable, Kajabi, Thinkific, and Kartra. You will also need appropriate module and class titles, a cover image, and a concise, well-written, accurate course description.

Online Series

Like the in-person specialty series mentioned on page 50, an online yoga series is a series of classes tailored toward a particular theme and, in this case, delivered online. They can be offered livestream or hybrid, and you can record the classes to also offer them on demand.

BENEFITS

- Students will commit to being part of a series that has a beginning and an end.
- A series gives the students a goal or outcome they

want to accomplish or a subject they want to learn about.

- You can build your schedule around your series, which is typically a four- to six-week commitment. You could offer a series in conjunction with a drop-in schedule, or if you have a committed following of students, you could offer a series throughout the year (quarterly, for example), as an alternative to drop-in classes.

- Along with that commitment, you'll also know what your income will be ahead of the series start, rather than being subject to the unpredictable nature of drop-in income only. If you're running the series yourself and handling the revenue, the income will be like an advance as it will arrive before or at the start of the series.

Keep in Mind

- Planning, producing, executing, marketing, and providing customer care for an online series requires a fair amount of administrative effort.

How to Integrate Online Series into Your Repertoire

To add this model to your teaching, consider the following steps:

1. Do some market research by polling your students on the topics that interest them and the format that works best for them.
2. Choose a compelling topic of interest to your community.

3. Decide on the format (for example, a four-week series meeting once a week or a six-week series meeting twice a week) and duration of the classes.
4. Price the series.
5. Have an e-commerce system set up to take payments.
6. Choose a meeting software such as Zoom to host and record the livestream classes.
7. Set up a platform to host the recorded videos.
8. Use appropriate class titles, a high-quality cover image, and concise, well-written, accurate descriptions.
9. Market and launch your series and be prepared for ongoing marketing efforts.
10. The day before the series begins or the day of, remind registered students when class is starting and provide the access link.
11. Teach the series live, record your sessions, and upload them to your hosting platform.

Online Teacher Trainings

An online teacher training is a formal certification program that can be completed online. It's a much longer, more complex version of an online course, with a definitive effort to build community among the participants. Many are hybrid versions in which a certain percentage of the required hours is completed online (usually a combination of synchronous and asynchronous learning) and a certain percentage happens in person, either at a yoga studio or in the form of one or more retreats.

Note: teacher trainings should be led only by very experienced teachers who are extremely well trained in designing curriculums of study.

Benefits

- Online trainings are accessible to students who otherwise could not afford the time and expense of traveling to a training.
- It can be easier to fill an online training course because of the above benefit.
- Online learning can be more effective than in-person learning because it gives students full control over their studies by letting them work at their own pace. For example, after watching asynchronous content, they can bring their specific questions to the live sessions, which enhances their understanding. Students can also replay classes to review and absorb the teachings even further.

Keep in Mind

- While online learning has its advantages over in person, when it comes to yoga teacher training, certain things are best performed in person, such as teaching hands-on assists and being able to witness how a teacher trainee moves through a room of students and teaches to who they see, rather than teaching to squares on a gallery screen display.
- Planning, producing, executing, marketing, and providing customer care for an online teacher training requires a substantial amount of administrative effort.

How to Integrate Online Teacher Trainings into Your Repertoire

Getting deep into the highly detailed, step-by-step process of executing an online yoga teacher training is beyond the scope of this book, and every teacher training is different, but here are the main steps you'll need to plan for:

1. Determine whether there is demand for yoga teacher training in your community.

2. Develop a comprehensive curriculum and then decide which elements are best recorded for on-demand/asynchronous consumption and which are better delivered live/synchronously.

3. Create a budget with projections on different attendance scenarios and tuition options based on going rates, and price your training accordingly.

4. Consider scholarships and payment plans to make the training more affordable for students who need assistance.

5. Decide on dates, duration, and format.

6. Create a downloadable training manual.

7. Consider including assistant teachers or support faculty who can facilitate smaller group cohorts online between sessions to review content, progress, and practice-teaching.

8. Build your infrastructure, which will include an e-commerce system to take payment and an organized LMS such as Teachable, Kajabi, Thinkific, or Kartra.

9. Create an application form in Google Forms or another form builder so you can vet applicants.

10. Launch the training marketing campaign and begin the ongoing marketing process.

11. Because this is a higher-ticket item, make yourself available for "sales calls," which give you an opportunity to speak directly with prospective students, ask questions, get to know them, and determine whether the training is a good fit for them.

12. Film your on-demand content in advance of the training.

13. Execute the live parts of your training and publish your on-demand content in your LMS.

Teaching for a Large Yoga or Fitness Platform

There are several competing online yoga and fitness platforms that have a faculty of yoga professionals as part of their team of content creators. Some names you may have heard are Yoga International, Glo, Wanderlust, Yoga Journal, and Peloton. While once reserved for well-known teachers, most of these platforms are aiming to improve representation among the teaching team and are striving to bring on teachers from diverse backgrounds as well as those that cater to niche audiences — including those less well known to the general public.

BENEFITS

- If the class location is chosen by the platform, you get to be a teacher, not a producer — all production is done for you, and equipment is provided.
- Larger platforms have large distribution, which gives you great exposure to yoga students all over the world.

- It can be challenging to get contracted on the larger platforms as they typically have a full roster of teachers already.
- Platforms will more readily hire yoga teachers who already have reach, whether that be a large email list or a substantial social media following, so the platform can grow its membership base.
- Some platforms will want you to film remotely from home, in which case some of the production effort will fall on your shoulders. They might provide equipment for you, or there could be an expectation that you provide basic equipment.
- To maintain good standing and to be asked back to film, you will need to be open to marketing your classes, be on point for marketing collaborations with the platform, engage on the platform's social media accounts, and be pleasant to work with, coachable, and well prepared ahead of filming days. (These are not necessarily cons, but considerations, to be sure!)

HOW TO GET HIRED ON A YOGA OR FITNESS PLATFORM

Getting hired on a larger yoga/fitness platform is a matter of being in the right place at the right time. Networking and relationship building with people associated with these platforms is one way to get yourself visibility and a possible invitation. Visibility is key, so make sure you are teaching in-person classes, attending yoga events, building your email list and social media pages, and generally putting yourself out there.

Online Private Lessons

Teaching private lessons online became quite popular during the pandemic and has remained a viable way to connect with students one-on-one or in small, semiprivate groups. They're typically done through Zoom or Google Hangouts.

BENEFITS

- Your student doesn't have to go anywhere to meet you, and vice versa.
- Private lessons are a great way to earn a higher hourly rate, even online.
- You can record your lesson via the meeting software (for example, Zoom or Google Hangouts) and send the student the video for continued reference.
- Depending on how savvy your student is with positioning their camera, you can get new and clearer perspectives of their body that you wouldn't get in person. I discovered this working with a student who put her laptop on the floor — a place I would never put my face — and when she did, I was able to see her feet in a way I would never otherwise have seen. As a result, I was able to give her feedback on how to adjust her feet to help relieve some discomfort she was having in her knees!

KEEP IN MIND

- With online there can be no hands-on assists, which are typically a hallmark of private lessons.
- If your student doesn't have a strong broadband/wifi

connection, glitches can impact your ability to communicate.

- It's generally more challenging to observe your student without a 3D view.
- Students are responsible for their lighting, camera setup, background, and audio, so you may need to give them some initial technical coaching to enable you to see and hear them clearly.

How to Integrate Online Private Lessons into Your Repertoire

Building an in-person private clientele is covered on pages 51–52. Building an *online* private clientele is quite similar but can be more challenging. Many yoga teachers acquire new private students in the moments after class when students ask questions about something in their own practice and the teacher suggests working privately. Clearly with online classes, those intimate opportunities to connect are generally not an option. Still, the largest source of private yoga referrals comes from word of mouth. So once you have one or two satisfied online clients, they will tell all their friends!

Logistically, you'll want the following components in place to do business with a private client:

1. An e-commerce link to send to your student for payment ahead of the session or right afterward. If they are buying multiple sessions in bulk, they can pay in advance with the appropriate payment link. Some popular examples of services you can use to get paid include Union.Fit, PayPal, Venmo, Zelle, or Punchpass.

2. An account and proficiency with a meeting service like Zoom or Google Hangouts.

3. The capability to record your session and send it to your student afterward, as a bonus option included in the lesson price, as mentioned above.

4. Ability to use the screenshot feature on your device when you want to highlight your student's alignment to capture what you're seeing in their pose. Then you can send them the screenshot(s) for reference during the session or simply use screen sharing in your meeting software to show them the screenshot you took. This is the online equivalent of looking in the mirror in person together while the student is in a pose and pointing out what you see while they are looking at themselves too.

Teaching for a Yoga Studio That Offers Online Classes

If a studio you work at offers an online component to their services, you might either teach from your home as part of their teaching schedule or offer hybrid classes, livestreaming your in-person classes so students can tune in from home. Offerings could include drop-in classes, on-demand practices, courses, series, private lessons, and more.

BENEFITS

• Either the studio handles production and administration, freeing you up to simply teach, or you share in the responsibilities, which takes some of the pressure off you.

• You're involved in an established community.

- You can use the studio's reach and distribution instead of having to generate that solo.

Keep in Mind

- Since the studio has overhead and is doing a lot of the work, plus bringing in the students, you'll be sharing the revenue instead of earning 100 percent of the revenue as you would if you were running things solo. But the lack of administrative responsibilities does save you time, so the trade-off may be worth it.
- A studio may impose a certain style of teaching that doesn't match your way of doing things. You will need to decide if that's a deal-breaker for you or just fine.

How to Integrate Teaching for a Studio Online into Your Repertoire

Acquiring teaching positions for hybrid classes at a yoga studio is likely to be an organic extension of the in-person classes you're already leading at that studio. Be sure to show enthusiasm for teaching hybrid style (if indeed you're grateful for the opportunity) and some production acumen so studio managers know they can count on you to handle some of the tech side of things, as well as make the folks at home feel included.

Teaching on YouTube

Many yoga teachers post free video yoga classes on YouTube and maintain a YouTube channel. Having a YouTube channel is much like having a social media following, only your posts are in the form of videos with descriptions underneath.

Benefits

- YouTube enables you to earn decent revenue from ads, based on the number of ad impressions viewed on your videos.
- Having a robust channel can give you exposure to a large audience, which can increase your name and brand recognition.

Keep in Mind

- Although you can make money from ads, impressions for your videos need to be in the thousands of views at minimum for a meaningful return.
- YouTube is extremely crowded with an audience that is habituated to free content, which means that if you want to charge money for your services, people may not be interested in buying.

How to Integrate Teaching on YouTube into Your Repertoire

Once you've set up an account on YouTube, start posting videos! Promote your videos and your YouTube channel on your other platforms, including email newsletters and social media.

Online Yoga Production Equipment and Setup

Now that we've covered the terminology and the various business channels for teaching yoga online, let's get into the how-tos for teaching and producing digital content.

A question we get a lot is, How important is it to have polished production quality in digital yoga offerings? High-quality production means having great lighting that makes it easy for students to see the teacher; an attractive background or "set"; excellent sound, which makes it easier and more pleasant to hear the teacher's instructions; and overall video quality, meaning crisp, in-focus composition with a pleasing look and feel.

Having high production quality can be a factor that helps you stand out in the crowd of so many other digital offerings. However, it can take more time and effort, and significantly more financial investment, to produce at that level. Since your *teaching content* is the most important part of your offering, it's better to put out imperfectly produced content that can be created and published quickly than a single video that took weeks to prepare, edit, and post. In other words, don't let the perfect be the enemy of the good. Better to get your teachings out to your community efficiently and often!

On the other hand, if the quality is so poor that users can't hear what you're saying, or the lighting is so low that you are barely visible, you'll want to upgrade your setup and think twice before broadcasting classes that would frustrate the student. The question to ask yourself is, Does the quality of the audio and video distract from the teaching and overall experience, or does it enhance?

When it comes to production quality, do your best with what you have or make the appropriate investment in your business to get your content looking and sounding clear and pleasant to view, while not being so precious about quality that you never put anything out.

Before filming a class, it's always a good idea to check your composition, mat placement, lighting, and so on, and even do a test recording to make sure the quality is adequate. If you're filming on-demand content, do a test recording of yourself and then review the playback. If you're doing a live-stream, open the meeting before everyone arrives to check the quality.

The aim is to make sure you appear in contrast to your surroundings so the audience can clearly see you and hear you with crystal clarity.

Now let's talk about production equipment that can help create quality videos.

Cameras

You've got to have a camera if you want to shoot videos for yoga! You have a few camera options for filming online content:

- *Internal cameras:* The great news is that modern laptops, smartphones, and tablets all have internal cameras that can be used during livestream Zoom meetings to record your classes. The quality of videos captured with these sorts of cameras will be good enough, but you may require external lighting sources to make them look brighter and crisper.

- *Webcams:* A significant upgrade to an internal camera is a high-definition or 4K+ definition webcam, an external camera that mounts to the top of your laptop or can be put on a tripod, connected by cord to your computer or device. This takes the place of your internal camera and typically can adjust for poor lighting and has wide-angle capability (to capture a larger area), greater depth of field, and greater overall crispness. You can also use the camera's app to zoom in or out and adjust the settings to find the right tone, contrast, and brightness.

- *Professional cameras:* If you wanted to go a step further for on-demand content, you could invest in an actual video camera with a body and separate lens that would sit on a tripod and record to a memory card. Because this would be for on-demand content, no internet is required, which helps, since streaming impacts video quality in general.

One Camera or Two?

Some teachers like to use two cameras: one that's close-up to show them when they are lecturing or as they are observing the students on the screen, and one that is farther away that captures them on their mat when they are demonstrating. Others use only one camera for all. In that case, the ideal is to set up the camera where you can be close-up to observe or lecture, then have space to move yourself back to your mat when you need to demonstrate. This is a matter of preference and also budget. Clearly there's an added cost to having a second camera, as well as a certain amount of technical savvy and added complexity. With two cameras you'll have a bit more setup involved, and you'll need to know how to switch cameras using your meeting software settings. Personally, I've found that having two cameras enables me to enhance the level of detail in the online experience, and I've become fairly dexterous in switching back and forth when needed.

Camera Setup

Be mindful of how you frame your yoga videos. For best results, keep the camera at a neutral height, not too high or too low, so that the camera is aiming at you head-on so as not to distort your body (more on ideal camera placement in the list below). You may also want to run a test recording to make sure your camera angle(s), focus, and lighting are to your liking.

Most teachers use one of these two primary setups:

- *Lecture setup:* This setup is used when you're giving a dharma talk or a lecture and for the style of on-line teaching called observation teaching, which we'll cover in detail in chapter 12. In this setup, the teacher sits close to the camera and appears to the viewers as a "talking head" that takes up most of the screen. In livestream classes held on Zoom or other video-conferencing software, the lecture setup enables the teacher to view the students (either as a gallery of squares on their screen or, when desired, individually) and give them feedback in real time. When using this setup, make sure your camera or device is positioned high enough that the lens is at eye level. Use a tripod with an attachment that accommodates smartphones or tablets, or place your laptop on a shelf or even a stack of books to get the camera elevated.

   Many make the mistake of sitting too far away or placing their device on a desk so that they must look down at the screen. This means that people see the bottom of your chin rather than looking at you head-on as though making eye contact.

- *Asana setup:* In this setup, used most often for demon-stration teaching (see chapter 12), the teacher is on their mat and demonstrating asanas for the students or practicing along with them. Position your mat so that the long side is facing the camera. This way, you can sit or stand in the center of your mat to address the students, and when you turn to the side for downward dog or standing poses, they will have a clear sideways/profile view of your body. Make sure the camera is far enough away that your entire body and mat are in the frame. Test this in a few positions: standing with arms overhead, seated or in pigeon pose, and lying on your back in supta padangustasana 2 with a leg extended out to the side toward the camera. If any part of your body gets cut out of the frame, create more distance between the mat and the camera.

Lighting

Good lighting is essential for visibility and clarity, and it can make a huge difference in flattering your facial features.

If possible, film in an area with lots of natural light. Be sure the light is shining on you, rather than behind you. For example, setting yourself up with a window behind you will make you appear backlit as a silhouette. Or if you have a window on only one side of the room and therefore have natural light pouring in from the side of your setup, you might want to invest in stand lights (available in camera equipment stores) on the opposite side to balance it out. Alternatively, you could get a large white foam board (available in most art or office supply stores) and place it on the opposite side to bounce the natural light back onto the darker side of your face.

It is possible, though, to have too much sunlight in the room, which can make you appear overexposed and "blown out." If this is the case for you, experiment with window treatments to tone down the light.

If you are in a low-light situation because of either the

space, the weather, or the time of day, you'll need to increase your lighting. For close-up filming, like meditation or lectures, setting up a ring light behind your camera will be sufficient. For asana classes where your whole body and mat setup are visible, a ring light will only work if you're in a small room, so it's better to get larger video lights mounted on light stands to illuminate sufficiently.

If you and your setup appear "grainy" on screen, add more lighting. If you look blown out, like you or your clothing are vanishing into the background, try using less light.

Also, create contrast. Be aware of how the color of your clothing relates to what's behind you. For example, if you have a dark-brown wall behind you and you're wearing black, you might blend into the background and be less visible on camera. If that's the case, you can either hang a white sheet behind you or simply change into brighter colors that contrast with the wall.

Last, consider the ambience you're aiming for, and adjust your lighting as needed. If you're recording a class for energy and stamina, you could purposely choose more vibrant lighting. On the other hand, if you're recording a restorative or before-bed evening class, you might choose to light more dimly with candles to set the mood for more relaxation.

Audio

One of the differences between online and in-person yoga classes is that online students tend to be more reliant on audio instruction than in real life. This is because they may be looking away from their screen to do the pose and therefore unable to see you modeling in 3D — it's hard to watch a video while moving on the mat. Students need clear audio instruction to facilitate practice. As such, poor audio quality can contribute to student drop-off. If a student is on their mat far from their screen and can't hear your voice well, they will likely disengage. Therefore, your audio quality is critical. Invest in high-quality audio equipment, and upgrade if needed.

The challenge with teaching yoga online is that you need to have some distance from the computer to be seen properly, but that means the mic in your laptop won't be able to follow you to your mat. Because of this, you will need an audio solution that allows you to speak while moving, no matter how far you stray from the camera. Here are the options:

- *Bluetooth headphones or earbuds* that are normally used to listen to music or talk on the phone can be used as a microphone and will enable you to hear unmuted participants in a live class meeting as well.

- *Professional equipment such as a headset or lavalier mic*, a wireless microphone pack you clip on your clothing, and a receiver that hooks up to the computer.

- *A podcast mic on a stand or a boom*, which can also be used to record audio-only meditations and lectures at your desk.

Always have a backup solution in case your audio equipment fails for any reason.

Mitigate background noise as much as you can. For starters, when choosing your practice and recording space, pick the quietest place possible. If you can hear background noise, such as traffic, planes flying overhead, family going about their business in the kitchen, construction, dogs barking, or other distractions, it's likely to be audible on your livestream or on-demand video.

If you can prevent external noises from happening during class, take action well before you start filming. For example, we bought a sign that we hang on our front door that says "Filming — Quiet on Set" so that delivery people know not to knock or ring the doorbell. Close doors and windows if necessary and eliminate mechanical noises such as loud fans.

For those noises that are out of your control, you can acknowledge them with your students. This makes your class all the more real and human, after all.

Students' Online Yoga Setups

Undoubtedly, your personal setup is critical to whether your students can see and hear you clearly. But what about your students' setups?

If you're teaching a livestream class or workshop, you may want to be able to observe the students and give them feedback, and you certainly will if you're teaching private lessons. To facilitate this, students must put some effort into making themselves visible to you. They won't have the same motivation to invest in professional production equipment, but many of the same tips on lighting and camera placement will apply to them.

PRO TIP

We ask our students to set up their cameras so that their mat is profile to the camera, with their left side to the camera when in downward dog. This way, when the student steps their right foot forward and windmills up into a standing pose like warrior 2, they are facing the camera ready for instruction, and they can see you. Since most instruction is given on the right side first, this allows you to give that instruction face to face. In addition, if all the students are facing the same way, you can more quickly observe the entire group and spot trends in their alignment, then address the trend with a demonstration.

When students register for our livestream programs and classes, we give them the following recommendations. You can send guidelines like these to students at the time of purchase, send them occasionally in your newsletters as a reminder, or post them on your website.

- *Choice of device:* Please join the meeting with only one device. If possible, we recommend using a device with a larger screen, such as a laptop or tablet, rather than a phone, so that you'll be able to clearly see the screen from your mat several feet away.

- *Choice of yoga space:* As best you can, given your home scenario, set up in a private, fairly open area where you can easily transition from lecture to asana. Pick a location with the most ideal lighting (whether natural or artificial) and set up with light shining on you rather than positioning yourself in front of a window where the light is behind you. If having a window or sliding door behind you is unavoidable, close any curtains or blinds to mitigate the backlighting.

- *Camera and mat orientation:* To enhance your experience and our ability to see and interact with you, set up your camera and mat so that your mat is profile (sideways) to the camera.

- *Camera distance:* Be sure that the camera is far enough away that it can frame your whole body in standing poses, with your arms up overhead (if your space is too small to permit this, position the camera as far back as you can to include as much of your body as possible), as well as poses down on the ground, like child's pose or pigeon.
- *Body orientation:* Position yourself on your mat so that your left side is to the camera when you're in downward dog. This way, you'll be able to see the camera when in a standing pose on the first side (with your right leg forward), and the teacher will have a consistent view of all students.

Preparing for Class and Minimizing the Risk of Tech Glitches

As incredible as video streaming technology is, technology gremlins seem to have a way of showing up at the most inopportune moments, causing stress, panic, and frustration. The power in your neighborhood can go out, or a crowded wifi network can cause video delays, video blur, or choppy audio.

While we can't ultimately control things like power outages, we can mitigate technology failure ahead of time and dramatically reduce its occurrences if we have backup precautions in place, such as the ability to pivot to a mobile phone on cellular (either as your camera device or as a wifi hotspot) or a battery backup to power computers and modems. Also, remember to periodically test all your production equipment for functionality and keep your system software and meeting software up to date.

Use a Preclass Checklist for Yourself

To prevent tech issues and have everything you need ready to go so you can focus on teaching, run through the tasks on the following checklist before class.

❑ Restart your modem and router.
❑ Restart your computer and any other devices before joining the meeting.
❑ Clear your cache and cookies (browsing data).
❑ Quit all unnecessary apps and close windows and tabs.
❑ Turn off wifi on as many other devices in your home as you can.
❑ Have a backup power supply if power loss is a concern.
❑ Make sure wireless audio equipment is charged.
❑ Make sure your laptop or other device is fully charged or, ideally, connected to a power source.
❑ Check camera setup.
❑ Mitigate background noise.
❑ Silence your phone and any other devices by putting them in airplane mode or "Do Not Disturb."
❑ Use the bathroom.
❑ Set up the props you need and prep your teaching space.
❑ Ensure that children and pets are occupied and can't interrupt class.

Publish a Tech Plan for Your Students

Send your students a plan to educate them on things they can do to prevent tech issues from interrupting your time together. You can send it at the time of purchase, send it occasionally in your newsletters as a reminder, or post it on your website. Here are the tips we share with our students:

❑ Keep your system software and meeting software up to date.

❑ Restart your computer or other device before joining the meeting.

❑ Restart your modem and router.

❑ Clear your cache and cookies (browsing data).

❑ Silence your phone and any other devices by putting them in airplane mode or "Do Not Disturb."

❑ Quit all unnecessary apps and close windows and tabs.

❑ Turn off wifi on as many other devices in your home as you can.

❑ Make sure your laptop or other device is fully charged or, ideally, connected to a power source.

❑ If you get kicked out of the meeting room, no worries. Stay calm and click the meeting link provided in your confirmation email.

Start Your Class Meeting Five or Ten Minutes Early

Getting ahead of tech issues before class starts allows you to catch up with your students and be social before beginning the session. Ask those present if they rebooted their computers, updated their meeting software, and silenced their phones. Make yourself available to answer questions and troubleshoot tech for them. There will be times when a student is unable to access the meeting or comes and goes due to glitches. Unless you have a dedicated team member who can help them, you're going to need to get your class going for the sake of the students who are present. Once class is finished, you can reach out to the student who had problems to help them troubleshoot and offer them the recording if they missed class altogether.

CHAPTER FIVE

Building Your Business

The practical business issues discussed in the next two chapters may not be new to you if you're already teaching. But if you're reading this book, I assume you want to build your business. Whether you're new to teaching or a veteran, and whether you teach in person or exclusively online, it's beneficial to understand these fundamentals and review them regularly.

Write a Business Plan

First of all, don't panic! The term *business plan* sounds formal, complex, and intricate, but it doesn't have to be. Simply put, a business plan identifies a demand in the marketplace and explains how you plan to fulfill it. My favorite guide is *The One Page Business Plan*, by Jim Horan. It's an easy-to-use workbook that helps solidify your plan and business.

As noted in chapter 2, you may not *need* a formal business plan unless you are applying for loans or seeking financial backing for a teaching business. But your business will feel more solid and professional when you take the time to write up even a simple plan.

Beyond putting a plan on paper, it is also useful to occasionally revisit your mission statement and core values. This helps keep you focused.

HIRE MONEY PROFESSIONALS

You can't hide your head in the sand — or up in a cloud — when it comes to taxes and bills. Unless you are gifted at accounting and bookkeeping, hand these tasks over to professionals. The right accountant and bookkeeper will help you make sense of all money matters including your taxes, knowing what you can write off as business expenses, and getting your bills paid on time.

Neglecting financial matters hurts your teaching in the long run. It can distract you with worry and, at worst, cost you time and money when you have to deal with mistakes and missteps. The best way to find a financial professional you can trust is by word of mouth: ask those closest to you for recommendations.

Build a Yoga Résumé

Keep an up-to-date résumé that describes your training, teaching experience, and special skills and attributes. Have it ready to send out (or to print out and deliver in person) whenever an attractive teaching opportunity arises. The networking site LinkedIn (which you may want to consider signing up for if you haven't already) has its own online résumé form that prompts you to key in relevant items.

List your educational history, including degrees and continuing education certifications. Give details of your yoga

training credentials, such as what teacher trainings you grad-
uated from and your main teachers. If you have a Registered
Yoga Teacher credential from Yoga Alliance, state the level
(RYT 200, RYT 500, E-RYT 200, or E-RYT 500).

For your teaching experience, outline how long you've
been a self-employed yoga teacher and describe the types
of teaching you've done: for example, "Self-employed yoga
teacher, 1997 to present, teaching private lessons, group
classes, workshops, retreats, specialty series, and teacher
trainings." Specify where you have taught and for how long. It
can be useful to tailor your résumé to reflect the values and
goals of the specific studio you're applying to. And be sure to
include any other skills you possess that are relevant to yoga,
such as physical therapy, nursing, psychotherapy, or massage.

Get the Best Teaching Opportunities

I interviewed studio owners and gym managers about how
they find their teachers. After doing so, I came up with a list
of what teachers can do if they want to pick up classes at a
particular studio.

The key is to be present and visible at your desired location. When you are out of sight, it's easy for you to be out of
mind. Studio owners and managers have a lot going on and
can easily forget about you, even though they might love to
have you on the team. Here are some ways to increase your
visibility and presence.

- Get on the substitute list by auditioning, if applicable, or dropping off a résumé.
- Guest teach and substitute teach as often as you can
  at the places where you want to work.

- Attend classes and events where you want to teach.
- Be friendly, helpful, and upbeat. Offer to put away props, fold blankets, or blow out candles at the end of class.
- Make time before and after class to have conversations and build relationships with the staff.
- When you teach as a guest or substitute, ask students at the end of class to recommend you if they enjoyed the class. Say something like, "If you enjoyed class today, please let the management know." This is not too much to ask, and it has worked for me every time. Tell your students how to submit the feedback if it is unclear. For example, you might suggest that they fill out a comment card or mention your teaching to a manager.
- Dress professionally on your way to and from the yoga studio. I suggest wearing regular clothes rather than yoga clothes; after all, you don't often see doctors walking around town in scrubs or white coats! Wear something in which you feel confident, professional, and successful. Activewear, while comfortable, does not exude professionalism.
- When you truly connect with a teaching venue, say so. Let the managers and staff know that you understand and agree with their values, vibe, and community. Let them know that you are a good fit for their establishment.

When starting out at a studio, you may have to agree to whatever teaching slots the management is willing to give you, but if you are patient and committed to both teaching and marketing, your classes will eventually fill and do well. My rule of thumb is to give it at least four to six months, even if your classes are small. The individualized attention you can provide in smaller classes turns into great word-of-mouth referrals. More important, over time the studio will recognize your efforts and offer you more favorable time slots, and you will feel more confident in asking for them.

When you want to be considered for a better slot at an existing location, here are some steps to take:

- Set a goal for filling the classes you do have, and take action (using the ideas in this book) to increase your student base. It can be frustrating when a time slot is less than ideal, but if you can do the best you can with the slot you currently have, you're more likely to get a better slot sooner.

- Continue to present yourself professionally. Make sure what you wear to, from, and in the studio is clean and looks fresh. This may be hard to do if you're racing around town teaching multiple classes, but a harried, disheveled teacher is hard to rally behind.

- Build relationships with the owners and staff by sharing incidents or issues at the studio they might want to know about. Do so in a supportive way. For example, you might overhear students talking in the changing room about how the studio always smells like sweat right after the 6:00 PM class when they walk in for your restorative class. This is feedback the studio needs to hear, and perhaps it's something that has been bugging you as much as it bugs the students. Relate the feedback in a way that conveys the facts without any emotions you might have attached. Suggest a solution, if you have one, and offer to help implement it.

- Be dependable, willing to work with the studio's vision, open to feedback, and appreciative when you receive feedback.
- Be proactive. Figure out what the studio needs from you and provide it to the best of your ability.
- Follow studio protocols, and if you're going to miss a class, find a good sub ahead of time.
- Be on time, be consistent, and don't miss too many classes.
- Clearly express the ideal class times you'd like to be considered for when they open up, but avoid coming across as impatient or entitled. Instead of saying something like, "I really thought I'd have better slots on the schedule by now," or, "I've been teaching here for two years — don't you think it's time for me to get a 6:00 PM class?," as you build relationships and become closer to the owners, share your vision of how many classes a week you see yourself teaching and what you want to offer your students. Share your vision, values, and mission statement.
- Work with everyone as a team to help the studio succeed, including your fellow teachers. Help build community and synergy.
- Always be gracious. Express appreciation and thanks to management and owners for the opportunity to work at the studio, gym, or spa. Do this even if you're not yet being paid what you think you're worth. Your positive attitude and gratitude will pay off.

RURAL BUSINESS BUILDING

Building a yoga community in rural areas can be challenging but, hey, so is yoga! Go ahead and set the ambitious goal of getting everyone in the area into yoga. You might begin by creating a Facebook yoga group for the area to get people talking about yoga, you, and yoga events in your area. Because many people may be new to yoga, be sure to offer accessible beginner classes. As you meet people, remember to add them to your email list and stay in touch.

Try to think of creative, community-specific ways to make your yoga classes must-attend events. Promote them as socializing opportunities for people who may live far apart. Honor someone or something significant in the area and allow students to network about what they do in the community.

Offering tea and light snacks after class is a thoughtful touch that recognizes some people may have traveled a long distance to get to class. Gestures like this count and help you stand out from other teachers. Make your class worth the drive. Respect your students' time by preparing thoroughly to offer classes that give them value.

Should You Quit Your Day Job?

No one ever said being a yoga teacher would make you rich — and if someone does say that, you should probably run away as fast as you can — but it is realistic to believe that yoga can provide a modest living for a single person or a supplementary income for a family. Considering that you may never have to work nine to five, sit in a cubicle, or answer to a boss, you can get by and be pretty happy in the process if you're able to support yourself through teaching.

The yoga lifestyle can be costly, though. Yogins often must travel and pay for continuing education. They tend to be conscious consumers who spend more to support local businesses and humanely and sustainably manufactured products. Like anyone else, they want to support and educate their children well. Many donate generously to good causes. Can a career as a yoga teacher really support this kind of lifestyle?

The answer is that it depends. Some yoga teachers living in urban areas can do quite well with a loyal student base at a popular studio and an affluent clientele who can afford private lessons. Others in different locations struggle to get by.

Once you know how much you need to meet all these expenses, create an annual teaching calendar (as described in chapter 3) and do some projections to estimate your annual income from teaching yoga. If your projected income falls short of your expenses, it's not yet time to quit your day job.

If your current job keeps you from putting 100 percent of your energy into your yoga career, it can be hard to know whether you could safely switch to teaching yoga full time. In this situation it is best to continue to refine your yoga teaching and business skills as a second career until you can be confident that you would do well as a full-time yoga teacher. The fantasy of roaming the world as a yogin, teaching, studying, and answering to no one, is not realistic. A good yogin is also grounded and practical. Bottom line? Don't quit your day job if it would mean putting yourself or your family on shaky ground.

Sustainable Teaching

Ideally, teaching yoga should be a career that enables you to do what you love while at the same time being able to *live*. An ideal teaching schedule allows ample time for your practice, personal development, leisure pursuits, and time with family and friends. It lets you teach at the times of day when you are most energized, and in locations that enable you to reach the student demographic you serve best and most enjoy teaching.

Often, however, the yoga teacher is more frazzled and unbalanced than their students! Trying to maintain an unsustainable teaching schedule can lead to burnout, resentment, lack of time for practice or professional enrichment, and financial difficulties. For new teachers, the temptation to say yes to every chance to teach can be counterproductive. And agreeing to teach for very little will undermine the market value for all yoga teachers — so be careful not to spread yourself too thin for little compensation.

Every opportunity involves trade-offs. Here are some factors to consider when deciding whether to pursue a teaching opportunity at a studio — or continue with your existing classes there.

- *Exposure and fulfillment:* Consider the studio. Do you like teaching there? Does it have a good vibe, or is there unresolvable tension? Are you nourished and fulfilled by teaching this particular group of students? Is the class size stable or growing? Are you getting good exposure to new students or teaching students who may want to take your workshops and attend your retreats in the future? If so, these factors may offset other potential disadvantages of the class location or schedule.
- *Location:* Traveling to inconvenient locations can be hellish not only for you but also for your students. If that's the case, everyone will be harried as they enter class. Travel delays that cause late arrivals make

everyone stressed and apologetic. Classes that are logistically challenging because of travel time or a shortage of parking won't be as well attended. Some of these disadvantages may be offset if the studio is in a location where you (and your students) can also run errands, get groceries, eat a nice meal, and work out at your favorite gym.

- *Payment models:* As mentioned earlier, studios typically pay either by the class or by the number of students. When you are first starting out and have not yet developed a student base, getting paid by the class is much more secure. However, when you are paid by the number of students, you have greater earning potential and have more incentive to promote your own classes.

- *Student base:* The overall number of students where you're considering teaching can affect your income. A studio with a large student base will be more difficult and competitive to break into. Although you may immediately start off with larger classes, more established studios have a huge number of teachers on their roster. At a newer studio or one with a small student base, it will take longer for you to build your own following, but it might be easier to get desirable teaching slots. So consider whether you can afford to earn less initially by teaching at a studio with a smaller base.

Optimal Scheduling

Long experience, good and bad, has led me to these general guidelines for establishing a productive, sustainable teaching schedule. They involve assessing both the needs of your clientele and your personal situation.

- Traditionally, students tend to prefer attending yoga class every other day with the same instructor for consistency. Be sure you can teach a class at least twice a week at any given studio or gym. Offer classes on alternate days (e.g., Monday and Wednesday or Tuesday and Thursday), in the same style, at the same level, and at the same time at each location. Classes held on consecutive days are not as popular.

- To reach a more diverse crowd, teach various levels of classes, including beginner classes, and teach both daytime and evening classes.

- Tailor your class schedule and offerings to the local community. You can do demographic research at city hall, look up census information online, or, more simply, observe the places where people are practicing wellness and fitness activities. Do you see mostly women? Men? Athletes? Elderly people? Are there mothers with children in day care or nursery school? Do you see professionals on a break from the office? When do you see the most people at the gym or wellness center? This information will help you decide which times of day are most convenient for students to attend yoga class, and what types of classes to offer.

- For efficiency, minimize travel between different studios.

- If possible, commit to the time slots when you can be most present and focused. If you're not a morning person, don't say yes to the 6:00 AM Sunrise Flow! And if you start to fade by 7:00 PM, say no to the Evening Simmer Down.

- Space your classes so that you have time during the day to eat, rest, practice, do errands, and schedule appointments.

- Schedule private lessons and meetings just before or right after your classes, while you are already out and about.
- Balance your teaching against other important personal commitments, such as date night, family time, yoga class with your favorite teacher, and weekend getaways.
- Miss class only when absolutely necessary. Consistency and presence are critical to the success of your classes. If you're continually having to find substitutes, you don't have the right schedule.
- Keep track of your energy levels. If you can't give your all in every class you teach, consider cutting back or rearranging your schedule.

Some other outside factors influence scheduling preferences. In an area flooded with young professionals and parents with young children, the best-attended classes are often in the late morning, after kids have been dropped off at day care or at school. Parents who need to pick up kids after school are unlikely to attend a 5:00 PM class. In a downtown area, you'll want to schedule classes around business hours: in the early morning, during lunch breaks, and after 6:00 PM.

Does class size matter? Of course a smaller class allows more individual attention, and the class can be more easily tailored to the students who are present. On the other hand, a full class is more energizing. We asked our graduates how they taught when the room was full versus sparsely attended in proportion to the size of the room. They said a full class flowed better and that the energy in the room made them more inspired, confident, and engaged. For me, the enthusiasm and increased energy of a full class draws the teachings out of me, and I even come up with new ways of explaining things, resulting in more student engagement. In addition,

I have always felt students have a stronger sense of community when they see a full room. Although you might prefer a smaller class with lots of space on the floor, consider how it makes the students feel as well.

A Sustainable Teaching Schedule: A Case Study

During the first "90 Minutes to Change the World" course I ran, one of the teachers asked for my help with her schedule, so I posted her schedule online for everyone to weigh in on. I called it a "fruit-salad schedule" because it was such a random mixture of offerings. It looked like this:

	TUESDAY	THURSDAY
6:00 PM	Level 1/2	Hatha 1
7:15 PM	Power Yoga 1/2	Hatha 2

She taught at a studio Tuesdays and Thursdays. At 6:00 PM she had a Level 1/2, followed by a Power Yoga 1/2. Then on Thursdays she taught Hatha 1, followed by Hatha 2. This schedule made it impossible for a student to attend the same kind of class at the same time every other day. In addition, the names of the classes were confusing: how is Level 1/2 different from Power Yoga 1/2?

Here is the schedule I proposed instead:

	TUESDAY	WEDNESDAY	THURSDAY
6:00 PM	Level 1/2	Power Yoga 1/2	Level 1/2
7:15 PM	Power Yoga 1	Level 2	Power Yoga 1

Scheduling a Level 1/2 class at 6:00 PM and a Power Yoga class at 7:15 PM on Tuesdays and Thursdays would allow students to attend the same-level class regularly. The additional offerings on Wednesday could be paired with Monday or Friday classes. This schedule is much more eye-catching and consistent. I recommend this same approach if you're teaching multiple online group classes each week.

Obviously, if you are an independent teacher, you are not always going to be able to convince the studios or gyms you work for to change their schedules to accommodate you. However, most studio managers want to know about your scheduling vision and may be willing to work with you as time slots open up and change. If you never share your vision, they won't know what you want!

In general, if you are doing very well in a slot, you have the leverage to ask for a schedule change. The irony, of course, is that you might not be doing well in a slot *because* you have a difficult time slot or fruit-salad schedule!

Every relationship with a studio owner or gym manager is going to be different. Be sensitive and tactful, understanding that they are juggling the needs of many teachers, the needs of their business, and their own personal needs.

Should You Open Your Own Studio?

When you've been running around town from class to class for a while, or teaching exclusively online from your home and missing the community of in-person classes, it's natural to fantasize about opening your own studio and having students come to you. Some people long to establish a place where their yoga community can come together. Whatever

your motive, if you find yourself considering running your
own studio, be sure to consider the pros and cons:

PROS	CONS
Control of your teaching environment	Burdens of supervising other staff, promoting your business, and managing a physical facility
Possible long-term returns on investment if you create a stable, profitable, reputable, and salable business	Financial risks of fixed studio expenses and uncertain revenue
Chance to create a yoga community	Legal complexities: employment laws, legal liability
Possibility of creating a self-sustaining business that will allow you to take time off occasionally without losing income	Doing your own marketing and promotion (rather than leaving it to the gym or studio manager)
Independence	More responsibility and stress

The decision to open a studio should be made with realistic and careful deliberation. You must determine whether
the area can support a yoga studio (or yet *another* yoga studio!) and whether there are suitable spaces available in your

area at a reasonable price. Ultimately the decision needs to come from your heart, and you must trust your intuition and inner guidance on what is right for you.

Once you've figured out what, where, and when you want to teach, the next step is getting the word out about your teaching. Most teachers don't enjoy self-promotion, but it is essential if you're going to make a living teaching yoga. In the next chapter we'll look at how to market what you — and yoga — have to offer, and hopefully learn to love doing it in the process!

CHAPTER SIX

Marketing Your Business

To serve its clients and grow, every business needs to get the word out about what it offers. But the more I talk to yoga teachers, the more I realize how much marketing is a sticky subject. This stickiness has its roots in two places. The first is the issue of how different people relate to yoga and the material world, as we discussed in chapter 1. The second is the notion that yoga students don't want to think about money: many see yoga as an opportunity to rise above the material and mundane.

Yoga teachers tend to internalize the idea that it's wrong to combine yoga and business. They frequently ask me things like, "Amy, if I put myself on Instagram practicing yoga poses, or create a brand and a website, doesn't that go against yoga's values?"

Yet if your goal is to be a professional yoga teacher and educator (rather than viewing yoga solely as a spiritual and personal quest) then it would behoove you to treat your teaching as you would any other professional endeavor that is financially compensated!

We know yoga improves health and wellness, can help reduce stress, and connects people to spirit. In practical terms, the results decrease health-care costs and even save lives. But if yoga teachers don't inform people about these benefits, how can people discover them? We have something powerful to share, and share we must! It's possible to get that message out with subtlety and elegance.

Spreading the Word about Your Services

Define Your Gifts and Goals

How do you teach most effectively? One on one? In small groups? To a room full of students? Do you work best with children, women, men, or people with special needs? Define your ideal students and craft your promotional materials and strategies to reach out to that kind of student.

Craft Your Unique Message

Once you are clear on your assets and goals, find a way to craft your message that is authentic and totally you — and make it classy. You can't go wrong if your message shares who you are and what you have to offer with sincerity. Your mission statement can be your guide. Given the ethics of yoga, crass marketing that artificially glamorizes or oversells you is not going to cut it. Instead of focusing on yourself, focus on the benefits that students will gain from working with you. Get feedback on your promotional material from close friends and students who know you well before making it public.

Confidently Send Out Your Offering

Be confident and enthusiastic in letting others know what you have to offer, knowing that you are providing a valuable service.

Publicize your offerings on a website; on social media platforms; through postcards, flyers, and business cards; and by email. Some people will like them, and some will not. You never know — your message might help change someone's life!

The Marketing Funnel

In business, a "marketing funnel" or "purchase funnel" is often used as a model of the theoretical journey of a customer toward the purchase of a product or service.

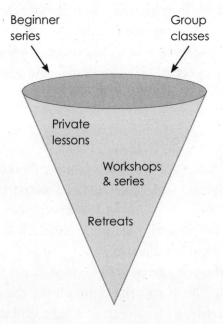

In yoga teaching, the top of the marketing funnel is the entry point to learning yoga. This could be as simple as a flyer for a yoga beginner series pinned on the bulletin board at a coffee shop, or your business cards listing private lessons that people pick up at their chiropractor's office. It could be a popular Facebook post about yoga put up by a yoga studio at which you work. Any of these might lead a beginning student to explore yoga.

As students fall in love with the practice of yoga, they become regulars at classes and begin to seek ways of advancing their practice. These offerings include special workshops, private lessons, specialty series, retreats, and, perhaps, teacher training.

The top of the marketing funnel needs constant attention to ensure a steady flow of new students. Think of it as a stream feeding a lake. If the stream dries up, the lake becomes stagnant. In yoga, this means that teachers are likely to be teaching the same yoga students as their peers are and face a dwindling student base. As existing students move, get sick, pass on, or occasionally lose interest in yoga, it's important to attract a steady stream of new faces.

Creating Your Brand

Brand is a tough word for yoga teachers (and their critics) to swallow. It sounds unspiritual and very corporate. However, if you think more deeply about it, knowing your brand is actually quite in line with yoga principles such as self-inquiry, self-knowledge, and authenticity.

One of the first exercises I give to students who take my training programs is to write down all the things they love about themselves, their talents, their gifts, and their positive assets. Yogins must be able to articulate who they are and their talents. This is not an exercise in narcissism: it is an exercise in knowing your assets so that you can more confidently and freely share your talents with the world. As my teacher Dr. Douglas Brooks once said, "It is a disservice to humanity and your community not to know and share your gifts." To know your assets (as well as your liabilities) is to know your brand.

You don't have to be — and can't be — everyone's yoga teacher. Match your gifts and passions with the student population with whom you want to serve. In other words, be yourself, and you will start to attract the kinds of students you most want to teach.

Knowing your brand, offering teaching that is consistent with your brand, and marketing as your brand actually reduces competition among yoga teachers. Many teachers simply copy what other "successful" teachers are doing, which results in overlap with those other teachers' offerings, instead of doing the self-assessment to gain crystal clarity about their own value propositions. If you are struggling to fill your classes, ask yourself whether you are clear about your brand identity and whether your promotional efforts reflect that identity.

The last time I did a branding inquiry for myself, I asked my students, family, peers, and friends to share words that came to mind when they thought of me. I got responses like *radiant, vivacious, generous with time, knowledgeable, organized*, and *real*.

I then thought about how those words could influence every aspect of my communication with the world, including my font and color choices, photography style, Facebook timeline, Instagram images, the writing style on my website, my bio, and workshop descriptions.

Think of some of your favorite brands or companies; Apple, Glo, prAna, Clif Bar, Lululemon, and Wanderlust are a few popular ones among yoga teachers we've polled. These names come to mind because they have a clear, recognizable image associated with desirable qualities.

You may not know exactly how to turn the words and

qualities you get from your own brand inquiry into your public face or brand. If you do have a good sense of graphic design and promotional writing, fantastic. If not, branding experts, graphic artists, and copywriters are in the business of turning your essence into a tangible presence. (If you reach out to them, consider offering to trade services with them.)

Know Your Target Market

Branding is as much about you as it is about the people who gravitate toward your style and brand identity. For example, because my brand is all about a caring approach to bringing ancient wisdom to modern yogins, along with a passion for environmental conservation, I tend to attract a target market of students who are seeking a yoga teacher they can believe in, one who cares about yoga's history and both its physical and its spiritual benefits. They see the bigger picture concerning health and whole living — mind, body, spirit — and they care about the world outside of themselves, the environment and the earth.

Once you've done the work to get to know yourself, the next step in developing your brand is to understand who the clients and yoga students are who will be attracted to your brand. If you don't know who your ideal client is, your marketing will be too broad to be effective. You need to make sure that what you're offering is a match for the audience that digs your teaching. If you do know your target market, it's much easier to build your brand identity. Knowing your students also allows you to offer a better product: your students will feel that your classes are customized especially for them. This cannot help but make them feel more fulfilled, happy, and accomplished in their practice. Giving your students what they want, helping them solve their problems and reach their goals, is like watching someone unwrap a present.

Knowing who your ideal clients are makes it easier to enjoy marketing and helps you succeed in attracting the kinds of students you love to spend time with. And teaching to people you resonate with is easier and more enjoyable.

To know and understand your students, you must see life through their eyes. Talk to them, ask them questions, listen to them, observe them, and compassionately put yourself into their shoes. Take the time to write down your thoughts about the qualities you want in your students.

The following exercise changed my entire way of teaching. It is partly this exercise that inspired me to create "90 Minutes to Change the World." Among other things, this exercise helped me understand what fellow teachers and teacher trainees might be seeking and how I could help them achieve their goals.

Answer the following questions for every kind of student or client you work with, including beginners, private clients, retreat clients, workshop students, group class students, online students, and teacher trainees. If you run a studio, you can do the same thing.

Getting to Know Your Ideal Yoga Client

1. First, build a profile of your current yoga students.

    a. What are the demographics of your current students (age, occupation, income, marital status, kids)?

    b. List what you know about the "psychographics" of your students: their lifestyle, beliefs, values, interests, and hobbies.

2. Now consider the demographics and psychographics of your *ideal* students. Answer the following questions from the perspective of an ideal student, as though you are seeing the world as that student sees it.

   a. What is your biggest dream, vision, or goal with respect to relationships, health, career, family, and/or general mindset?
   b. What is your biggest fear in developing a yoga practice?
   c. What are your favorite books, music, and TV shows?
   d. What magazines do you read?
   e. What blogs do you follow?
   f. What topics do you search for online?
   g. What conferences or events do you attend?
   h. What do you do in your free time?
   i. What other teachers or experts do you already follow?

Analyze Your Data

Completing this questionnaire is creative and fun but also serious work. Take your time with the exercise. If you get hung up on a particular question, move on. Some of this sort of thinking about your students is natural and intuitive; you may already be doing it in the back of your mind. But it is still worth trying to clarify those thoughts and get them down in writing.

When you think about your students' dreams and ambitions, they may include things like "Have a fulfilled life," "Feel connected to family," "Have a sense of well-being," "Be loved," and "Feel empowered."

What are your ideal students' biggest fears or worst-case scenarios for practicing yoga? They might fear embarrassment, injury, being singled out as not good enough, feeling pain, or standing out as stiff or old. Can you offer these students coping skills, alignment techniques to help them open up, your empathy and compassion, practical props, modifications, or humor?

When I look at the lists of responses created by yoga teachers in my "90 Minutes" course, I see numerous class theme ideas, plus an abundance of material that can be used on flyers, in social media posts, blog articles, workshop descriptions, and in bios and website copy.

This exercise can provide valuable material that will help you relate to your ideal students and clients — right from the heart. It can inspire everything you do to present yourself, both in your classes and in your promotional work (your website, social media posts, biographical sketches, and so on). Your confidence and ability to deliver teaching that hits home for your students will also increase dramatically.

Do this exercise separately for every kind of teaching you undertake, such as retreats, workshops, series, group classes, or private lessons, and apply it to every aspect of your overall marketing plan.

The Five Ps of Marketing

As you begin to think about marketing your offerings, it's handy to consider what are classically called the five Ps:

1. *Product:* In all your offerings — including group classes, private lessons, retreats, and series — what services and/or products are you promoting, and what is their value to participants?

2. *Price:* Consider what the going rate for this product is in the area where it will be offered.

3. *Place:* Are you in a market or location that can support you as a yoga teacher? Do people in your location want what you have to offer?

4. *Promotion:* How will you get the word out about what you're offering?

5. *Position:* How is your product — teaching — positioned in the overall market? What other activities are competing for your potential students' time and attention? Is your target student choosing between yoga and Pilates, yoga and fitness, or yoga and something else? In my area (Boulder, Colorado), most potential students are choosing between yoga and outdoor activities, so I take that choice into account in my promotions and scheduling by emphasizing the therapeutic benefits of yoga to the athletic body and the fact that our events take place after the sun is down or on weekends, when people have more time.

Creating a Yoga Marketing Plan

Having defined your own goals and mission and identified the client group you want to reach, it's time to consider how you will reach them to promote your services and talents. A marketing plan does not have to be a long, formal document; nor is marketing something you do once and forget about. It is dynamic and needs regular planning and attention.

Devote some time to your marketing planning and efforts each day. For each special offering you have scheduled over the next year, consider the first three Ps (*product, price,* and *place*) and then come up with at least two or three actions you can take toward *promotion* of the event that take *position* into account. Every time you plan a new offering and add it to your schedule, repeat this process. Here's an example — my marketing plan for a recent arm balances workshop:

MARKETING PLAN

Product: Arm Balances Workshop
Price: $60
Place: Studio, Boulder, CO
Promotion: Execute the following marketing plan, chunk each task into a calendar, and set reminders
Position: Competing with Pilates and outdoor activities

Website
Create event page on website (with e-commerce established).

Flyer or Postcard
Hire graphic designer and supply with content.
Print 500 copies.
Distribute in class and place in stores, gyms, coffee shops, etc., around town.
Leave a stack at the workshop venue.

Email
Mention in monthly newsletter for four months leading up to event.
Send out a dedicated email about the workshop one month before event, one week before event, and the day before event if space still available.

Announcements

Announce in all group classes and suggest to private
    clients.

Facebook

Create event page and invite friends — use arm bal-
    ance photo for the cover image.

Post every other week and interact on the event
    page for three months prior, and then once a
    week in the last month before event. Schedule
    posts ahead of time.

Time marketing posts with arm balance photos for
    Facebook page on same day as all emails, and
    set a $100 budget for boosting posts.

If relevant and appropriate, post about the workshop
    in community Facebook groups.

TikTok

Post a video every other week for three months prior
    to the event, and once a week in the last month
    before the event. Create and schedule posts
    ahead of time.

Instagram

Post once a month in the three months prior to event
    and then every other week in the last month be-
    fore event — use arm balance photo.

Don't feel you have to ace marketing all in one day. Break
it down into small steps and work at it consistently; schedule
marketing work into your day so you don't feel overwhelmed.
And remember that even one small effort — something like
letting class members know about other classes you teach —
can pay off.

Old-School Marketing:
Alternatives to Social Networking

In the next chapter, we offer advice about using social media to your advantage, and for most yoga teachers, it's an integral part of their marketing efforts. But despite social media's growing dominance, it still makes sense to have supplementary offline marketing strategies, which can be very effective in getting the word out about your services.

Augmenting your social media strategy with some tried-and-true marketing methods to increase your exposure among your student base and colleagues is a sure way to be successful as a yoga teacher and reach all audiences where they dwell. Here are a few suggestions for more-traditional marketing:

- Advertise your services in the local community wellness publication(s). In many towns and cities, these kinds of publications serve as a directory for alternative health practitioners. They are usually found in stacks at health food stores, cafés, and bookstores.
- Leave your business card or postcard in coffee shops, health food stores, and other establishments popular with people likely to be interested in yoga. Spend some time thinking about this. If you teach a class for elders or pregnant women, don't just think about where to find them; also consider where you might reach their friends, family, and caregivers.
- Ask for referrals from existing students and private clients.
- Maintain a current email list of your students and use email newsletters to stay in touch.
- Attend the conferences on health, wellness, and self-actualization that come through town. Even though

these events can feel huge and impersonal, they are places where you can connect with like-minded peers. I have met teachers who have influenced my work, vendors whose products I loved (and who might love my own future products!), and owners of retreat centers where I might teach. I've also had many conversations that have led to teaching invitations.

- If in-person networking makes you nervous, take a deep breath and introduce yourself to someone. Smile. Consider what it is they do, rather than what you do, and make a sincere comment, like "I love this aspect of your work," or ask, "How did you get into this work?" As the conversation progresses, you can find common ground to explain what you do. Your genuine interest or admiration should always be welcomed. If it isn't, that issue is most likely with them, not you.

CHAPTER SEVEN

Social Media

When I started teaching yoga, cell phones did not exist, let alone all the social media platforms available today. And given the speed at which these things seem to be moving, some of the platforms that are popular as I write — Facebook, LinkedIn, TikTok, and Instagram — may be passé when you read this book. In this chapter, I hope to offer advice that is valid for current social media platforms as well as for the new ones that are bound to come along.

Ironically, modern social networking is very much in line with yoga's centuries-old concept of connection, relationship, and union. Social networking brings people into dialogue across oceans. It lets big corporations communicate with far-flung customers, and it creates vibrant virtual communities. It offers forums where people can pour their hearts out, share their misfortunes, and ask for support in tough times. When tragedy or climate events strike, such as school shootings or wildfires and floods decimating whole neighborhoods, online communities mourn and take action together. Yet social media will only lean toward more positivity if we work to minimize the opportunistic, the unethical, and the predatory.

A WORD ABOUT EMAIL

Millions of people spend huge parts of their day addicted to social media platforms, but that doesn't mean the use of email is going away anytime soon. With email, you — not a big tech company — own your subscriber lists and your content. Conversely, if a social media platform fails or gets bought by a billionaire who runs it into the ground, you will lose access to all your followers and content on that platform. Not to mention, your email is not subject to a pesky algorithm that prevents people from seeing 80 percent of the posts you create. If a student wants to hear from you, they subscribe, and — voilà! — your newsletter lands in their inbox. Moral of this story? Build and give energy to your email list.

Why Bother?

Perhaps you feel that social networking will never be your thing, or perhaps you've tried it and, like many people, you're suffering from burnout from the endless feed of posts, tweets, and updates. The good news is that personal interaction will always remain an important way of letting people know about the good things you do. Indeed, face-to-face encounters are still the dominant source of word-of-mouth sharing, even more than online conversations.

That said, social media is also a form of word of mouth, but according to the book *Socialnomics* by Erik Qualman, it's word of mouth on steroids. He says, "Word of mouth is now *world* of mouth." While I used to tell yoga teachers that they could absolutely do fine without social media if they really wanted to remain offline, I've since changed my tune. Today, 50 percent of the world's population is under thirty years old, and 90+ percent of Millennials and Gen Z are on social media.

This means that most of this huge number of potential yoga students have embraced social media as a way of life. According to Qualman, Facebook has so many users that its "population" is now larger than that of China. Instagram and TikTok are not far behind. It's become clear that social media is not a fad but the biggest thing to change society since the industrial revolution. Unless you specifically want to teach yoga to a more limited population, my suggestion is to jump in and embrace social media.

For yoga teachers, social media — whatever the platform — serves two vital functions:

1. *Communication:* Keeping a conversation going about yoga in between classes and establishing yourself as a thought leader in the yoga industry
2. *Marketing:* Helping students find you and engage with your teaching

Old-school methods like flyers and newsletters do the same things, but the newer platforms make it all happen faster and make it possible to reach more people than ever before. Social networking is just another channel by which to communicate.

On social media platforms, you can converse with your students. They can ask you questions between classes. You can see pictures of their children and the activities they enjoy, and they can learn more about you as well. All of this results in a richer, more dynamic — and ultimately more personal — connection between you and your students.

FEEL THE FEAR ... AND DO IT ANYWAY

If you feel daunted by creating a presence on social media, ask yourself why. Is it because you lack technical skills, or because you feel you aren't worthy of being out there?

Or perhaps on some level you actually fear being successful? Maybe you aren't fully committed to being a yoga teacher or running a yoga business.

Strive to uncover the source of your fears. Bringing awareness to them is really the only way to get past them — and to claim your power to teach yoga successfully.

Many of us also suffer wounds to our self-esteem when our posts don't receive as many likes as we hoped, or our followers increase at a painfully slow rate, while our colleagues' seem to double in numbers every month. As with anything, if you become obsessive about numbers, you can lose sight of reality, which is this: you are a good person, you are a talented yoga teacher, you care about others, and you have much to offer, regardless of what your social media statistics look like! Take a deep breath and appreciate yourself from the deepest place of self-honor. Remember your greatness and your mission.

The Four Cs

Remember the five Ps of marketing in chapter 6: *product, price, place, promotion*, and *position*? Now marketers are embracing the four Cs of social media: *content, connecting, community*, and *curating*. Let's look at these in more detail.

Content

Sharing valuable content is the key to social media engagement. Is the content you are posting relevant to your target audience's interests, needs, and desires? What insights about yoga can you share with them?

Connecting

Have conversations, listen, and respond quickly to students' comments on social media. Your followers want to engage and learn from you, and when you nurture them, they are more likely to remain loyal to your brand.

To connect with your students, you also need to figure out which media platforms to use. Fortunately or unfortunately, yoga students tend to be on a variety of platforms. The most widely used are Facebook, Instagram, and TikTok, but specific categories of clients may be on different platforms, so you may have to manage multiple social media platforms. To find out who uses what, you can always survey your community!

Community

Social media provides community forums for both peer-to-peer communication and exchanges between peers and thought leaders. People look both to experts and to one another for help with their interests, issues, and needs. Creating forums for your students, whether via a Facebook group or a thread of comments on a blog, can be a great way to create and sustain a community around the practice. In addition, any engagement, whether it's likes, comments, conversations, or shares, is beneficial to the algorithm, therefore increasing the chance that your posts will be seen.

Curating

With still images and video now dominating social media, it's becoming more and more important to curate content, almost like managing an art gallery. Instagram users, for example, work hard at presenting photos on their grids that conform to a consistent type of photo or color palette. In addition to making sure your content is presented in an aesthetically appealing way, it's important to curate your posts for your distinct audience, so that the majority of posts are about sharing insights, useful information and links, personal stories, new insights, and fun photos and videos rather than being strictly promotional.

Social Media Basics

When you're ready to dive in, consider taking an online social media course to sharpen your skills. I have used the social media courses offered on Coursera.com as a resource to stay current. Many influencers who successfully built their own accounts now offer their own online courses and coaching programs to help others do the same. These may be helpful and educational as you learn more as well. Check out the latest trends and changes by reading current articles about the various platforms. Ask your peers, students, friends, and family about the networks they use and how they use them. Ask what kinds of posts they appreciate seeing and what rubs them the wrong way.

Here are a few tips for using social media platforms to get the most exposure for your content and business. We'll look at specific platforms in a moment, but these basic guidelines apply to using any social media platform:

- *Stay consistent.* If you venture online, stay active. Having an outdated or unused social networking account is like having an 800 number that no one answers. Set a regular schedule for posting on each platform that you know you can adhere to. If you can post three times a day on certain platforms, great. If you can't, pick a realistic schedule of days and times for posts to keep your followers engaged.

- *Create a bio "for the people."* How you write your bio can make the difference between someone quickly deciding to follow you vs. scrolling by. Most people list a bunch of words that describe their identity, such as, "Author, yoga teacher, mama, avid gardener," but that doesn't tell the prospective follower what's in it for them. Instead say who you are in your title. Then in the body of the bio list what you offer and what kind of people you offer it to, followed by a call to action (such as a link to sign up for your email list). As an example, here's my bio:

  Amy Ippoliti | Yoga + Wellness Educator
  🧘 Yoga 4 longevity
  🧘 Yoga teacher trainer @vesselify
  🌏 Rousing humanity to live as regenerative consumers
  🦶 Subscribe for 1 week free yoga
  linktr.ee/amyippoliti

- *Keep your posts short.* Although lots of people still read long novels and magazine articles, we've come to expect online communications to be short and sweet. The phenomenon known as microblogging is common on

Facebook and Instagram. Posts and photo captions become like tiny blogs.

- *Provide great content.* If you consistently provide useful and relevant content, whether it's your own material or shared from other sources, your followers will look to you as a resource.

- *Curate your posts.* Post content that's consistent with your mission and core values. This will reinforce your brand over time.

- *Promote sparingly.* While it can be tempting to post only about your events and offerings, marketing posts do not receive as much engagement and can also cause people to unfollow you. On Facebook, for example, unengaging posts can also negatively affect your page's score in the Facebook algorithm, resulting in your post having little or no visibility in people's feeds. By contrast, your engaging content-oriented posts will keep your page's score high so that when you do market your offerings, people will actually see them!

- *Engage, engage, engage.* Heavy engagement on your posts helps their organic reach. Therefore, as soon as possible, answer people's comments and get conversations going on your post. Leaving likes and comments on other accounts' posts also gives you more visibility, which can lead to more followers. Be prompt in answering direct messages (DMs) to help keep you connected through the algorithm with people who are engaging with you.

- *Facilitate sharing.* Enable the Share buttons or set the defaults on your website and blog so that other people can pass along your content. Getting your posts and

pictures shared, liked, retweeted, or repinned is the key
to building your contacts. A bigger contact list helps
you let more people know about the great work you do.
* *Have fun!* Social media is about networking and communication. If you're enthusiastic about engaging
with your network, your posts will reflect it. This is
your chance to spread your love of yoga.

Popular Social Media Platforms for Yogins

LinkedIn

LinkedIn is a site for professionals rather than purely for social
networking. Having a detailed profile on LinkedIn is like having
your best résumé online, accessible to those in your field at any
time. If you want to be considered a yoga professional, no other
networking site is more important. LinkedIn offers networking
groups where yoga teachers can collaborate on professional
matters. More important, it's a key site for contacting human
resources managers to promote your workplace yoga offerings
and for posting about the importance of yoga in the office.

Facebook

If you're comfortable with using Facebook and think it can
help build your teaching career, we recommend creating a
professional business page in addition to a personal profile.

To join Facebook, everyone has to create a personal profile page. This allows you to share details of your personal
life with your Facebook friends. Who those friends are is up
to you. Since you can have up to five thousand friends, many
small business owners use their personal profile page for
business as well, and add their clients as friends. However,

this approach requires careful monitoring of what is posted there, by you or any of your friends. If someone shares those embarrassing pictures of your late-night dance party or your awful high-school yearbook photo, your yoga students can see them too! Therefore, it could be better to keep your personal profile page truly personal, friending only people who are real-life friends and family, not clients or friends of friends.

Because Facebook does not want you to use your personal profile page to market your business, the company has created special features for business use. A professional business page can have unlimited likes (or fans, as the feature was once called). Anyone who likes your page can see the content, so you need to be judicious about what you post there.

FACEBOOK TIPS

- *Start liking other businesses' and colleagues' pages*, especially those of businesses that serve an audience similar to yours.

- *Engage with posts you like.* Check your news feed to see posts from the pages you like, and make a habit of commenting, liking, and sharing their content. This increases your visibility and means that followers of those pages may like your page, especially if you offer insight, humor, or helpful information in the comments.

- *Create Facebook event pages* to showcase your workshops, beginner series, retreats, and other offerings using the event page creator. Include all the specific details about the event and explain why people should attend. Event pages give people the chance to learn about the event and interact with other attendees. The sole disadvantage is that you can only invite your Facebook friends (meaning your personal page friends) individually to join the event. Therefore to get the word out to your business page followers, you must post on your page or in relevant Facebook groups you belong to, asking people to visit the event page and RSVP if they plan to attend. Any posts made to an event page will pop up more reliably on the feeds of those who have been invited or have RSVP'd.

As you may have noticed, Facebook has changed its algorithm so that unless your post is organically engaging, it won't make it into people's feeds, to the dismay of many. As I mentioned, marketing posts generally are not as engaging as more personal content posts, and Facebook knows this. Therefore, they have forced businesses to boost their posts and pay to have them show up in people's feeds. This is why event pages are such a great work-around.

- *Don't be shy.* Nobody is being forced to look at your page, so you should never feel that you are being pushy or "spamming" other people. However, do be mindful of the fourth C of social media and *curate* your posts so that they emphasize content over promotion.

FACEBOOK AND ME

I was late to the game when I joined Facebook in 2009. The whole first month, I was a "lurker" because I was terrified of people seeing or interacting with me. Even though I was already known in the yoga world,

I felt shy. This mode of communicating was new to me, and I was unsure of the consequences of posting or commenting. I was already inundated with emails and certainly didn't want more work.

I took baby steps to interact and found myself enjoying the connections with my students and others. Eventually, I started seeing a drop in the number of emails I was getting because I was communicating easily with lots of people on Facebook. It *is* a different way of connecting, often terser and more informal, but it is a connection, and it can be fun.

Instagram

You probably already know what Instagram does: it allows you to share photos, videos, and Reels online and to dress them up by applying filters that give the images a look similar to old-school Polaroid images or photos from a Kodak Instamatic film camera, as well as offering all the modern features of the best photo apps. You can use a variety of hashtags to categorize the images so that they will come up in viewers' searches.

This highly visual social media platform has become hugely popular with yoga enthusiasts. It abounds with pictures of creative evolutions of ever more advanced asanas, posted by yogins all over the world. Instagram offers a fine example of the pros and cons of online promotion. Viewers might ask, "What's with all these incredibly advanced yoga selfies?" or "Can I do yoga without doing *that*?"

So how can you use Instagram for a yoga business? The key is to use images and videos to tell a story — about what you teach and who you are, about your brand and the people or studios you work with. Think like your client. What can a photograph or video tell them about your services?

INSTAGRAM TIPS

- *Show pictures and videos of the studios where you work.*
- *Give viewers a backstage pass.* For example, take a picture of the books you have open when you're preparing for class, your notebook with stick-figure drawings of the class, and your feet sitting in sukasana on your mat as you're doing all this.
- *Document a day of teaching yoga* and include students in the footage. (Be sure to get the students' explicit consent before posting their photos.)
- *Share travel photos.* When you travel, especially for yoga training, workshops, or retreats, share photos and videos from the start of the trip to the end. Take your online audience along!
- *Use up to thirty relevant, specific hashtags.* Research hashtags that are trending (meaning popular at the moment, yielding numerous images in a search) and use them in relevant photos.
- *Let people in on some of the more mundane aspects of your life,* such as your morning rituals, favorite meals, or harvests from your garden. Or include your audience in aspects of your practice, such as sitting down at your altar to meditate or picking an oracle card.
- *Make Instagram Reels.* Consider learning how to use Instagram's engaging video maker to make Reels, videos that are up to ninety seconds. At the time of this publishing, Instagram gets Reels in front of people who don't necessarily follow you, so it's a great way

to build your following. Leverage trends by looking at the Discover Page on Instagram and incorporate popular audio (music or sound effects) and hashtags into your Reels.

- *Socialize and leave comments on others' posts,* especially around the time you publish one of your own posts, since the added engagement will trigger the algorithm to put your post in front of more accounts.
- *Curate your Instagram feed.* Having a well-planned grid that clearly showcases who you are will help convert profile visitors into followers. Consider how your grid looks as a whole — the color palette and what impression it gives when someone lands on your profile for the first time. If you want people to attend your yoga classes, make sure you actually have posts about yoga on your grid (in addition to the occasional view into your breakfast or your puppy's cuteness). You want visitors to immediately understand what your account is about and what's in it for them.

  To help with visually planning your grid and creating a consistent aesthetic for your feed before you post, use one of the various third-party Instagram feed planner apps.
- *Use keywords in your bio and captions to help with SEO* (search engine optimization) so your account and its posts come up in online searches. Instagram now allows searches via both hashtags and keywords.
- *Use Instagram Stories.* Stories allow you to share snippets of your life quickly and easily, and all Stories are highlighted at the top of the Instagram feed for free.

  Even though Stories only last for twenty-four hours, you can extend that life by pinning select stories in "highlights" on your profile so your visitors can play them again and again. This is great for featuring upcoming events, product partnerships, and online programs.

A WORD ON SOCIAL MEDIA YOGA FAME

While this book was being written, a new phenomenon in the yoga world emerged: the "Insta-famous yogi" or Instagram yogins. Yoga hobbyists, new yoga teachers, and veteran teachers alike have jumped on the Instagram bandwagon, posting photos and videos of their practice — each one more bendy and acrobatic than the next. The imagery is artistic and often shot with beautiful backdrops, such as beaches with cerulean blue water, mountaintops, and dramatic urban landscapes.

On the plus side, all this yoga sharing has brought the global yoga community together, friendships have been forged in real life, and many people have decided to try yoga for the first time after being inspired by these posts. On face value it offers a platform to share ideals, values, and lessons in life.

Like many using Instagram, yogins are taking advantage of the plethora of filtering apps available that not only help make their photos pop aesthetically but also can smooth skin, whiten teeth, and reshape body parts. The less you wear, and the deeper you bend, the more followers and more fame you might have.

Brands hoping to break into the yoga world are willing to pay yogins with large accounts to post about their products. A few yoga teachers are even earning more through endorsements on Instagram than they are from teaching, resulting in some controversy!

Are the teachers merely selling ad space on their accounts, or are they endorsing products they truly believe in sharing?

A more global concern is how social media fame is impacting the yoga world, in particular *studentship* among yogins. Impressionable yogins are starting to confuse fame and big followings for excellence in yoga and yoga teaching. "Insta-fame" is not necessarily the equivalent of being well educated, seasoned, wise, accomplished, or professional, and it's not a substitute for the years of study, perseverance, and patience it takes to be a yogin. You can only be as good a teacher as you are a student.

TikTok

TikTok is a popular social app where you can create, watch, and share short-form (up to three-minute) videos. Featuring personalized feeds of quirky videos set to music and sound effects, it has an addictive quality and high levels of engagement. There's a lot of dancing and lip-synching in the videos. TikTok's algorithm is particularly sophisticated in predicting what kind of content a user most likes, and dishes it out through its "FYP" or "For You Page."

Whether you're an amateur or a professional creator, the app allows you to add effects like video and audio filters, background music, text, and stickers to your videos, and users can collaborate on content and create split-screen Duet videos despite being in different locations.

Though TikTok's format lends itself to comedy and entertainment, more and more it's being used for "infotainment."

Popular topics include beauty, fashion, personal finance, and cooking, and not surprisingly, yoga videos are also gaining traction.

If you search for the word *yoga* on TikTok, the first videos that appear are close-ups of the crotches and butt cheeks of flexible young women in string bikinis flouncing their stretches to music. These types of videos are not about yoga teaching or yoga practice; they're about getting likes and followers. On a brighter note, in the midst of the dancing and lip-synch videos on TikTok, there's a subspace for yoga creators who are sharing their enthusiasm for the practice through instructional pose breakdowns, prop use tutorials, yoga challenges, partner poses, and touching clips about their progress on the path.

TikTok Tips

- *Identify your target audience.* Once you know what kind of people you want to attract and what interests them, create content specifically for that audience.
- *Educate your followers.* Create videos that teach people about what you do (yoga, meditation, pranayama, etc.), your services, and any recommended products. Teach to your target market, and give them information on how to make their lives easier through what you offer.
- *Cross-promote your videos.* Cross-promote your Tik-Tok content by sharing your videos on other social media platforms, in your newsletters, or on your blog. If you're sharing a TikTok to Instagram, just be sure to use an app that can remove the TikTok watermark

so your content on Instagram looks native to the platform.

- *Be mindful of what time of day you post.* You want to post when your followers are actively using TikTok. This can take some trial and error, but there are also TikTok scheduling apps widely available in the app store that can help you with when to post based on your data insights.
- *Engage with other TikTok creators.* Like all social media platforms, TikTok is about collaborating and connecting with others. When you engage with other TikTok creators (using TikTok's Duet and Stitch features as well as commenting), you will increase engagement.
- *Create and participate in TikTok challenges.* TikTok is full of challenges. The best bet is to participate in the same TikTok challenges that your target audience is active in. You can also start your own challenges.
- *Leverage TikTok trends.* Trends on TikTok include audio, hashtags, and sound effects. Do a search on the Explore page to find what's trending, and then use those same trends in your videos.
- *Use hashtags in an impactful way.* Hashtags help people find content that they're interested in. Hashtag use on TikTok can help you build your TikTok audience. Use a combination of trending hashtags, yoga-specific hashtags, and general hashtags that are relevant to what's in your video.

I was about to start writing about Pinterest, essentially a giant online bulletin board where you can "pin" and share images that interest you, and Threads, the microblogging app that arrived on the scene in summer 2023, but I realized that if I kept writing about different social media platforms, this chapter would go on forever. So let's stop here and return to general social media advice that you can adapt to any new platform that comes along.

Being Personal in Your Professional Posts

Social media has changed the way we present ourselves professionally. Prospective students now expect to be able to check out a yoga teacher online, through tweets or Facebook status updates, before even attending a class. While you might feel uncomfortable about airing parts of your personal life online in this way, it's part of doing business today. In my public posts, I certainly don't put any words or photos out there that I'd regret, but I do share snippets of who I am, what interests me, and what I think might inspire my readers. For example, on the next page is a post I made on Instagram about how my practice had evolved in recent years. Even though it wasn't a professional photograph, the post was personal and honest, so it received more engagement than other, less personal posts.

Because social media is interactive and is a two-way exchange, it also offers ways to gain valuable information and feedback. Clients and customers have easy and open methods of sharing positive feedback and gratitude, whether it's a like on Facebook or a detailed five-star review. On the other hand, of course, businesses are also much more vulnerable to negative feedback and even harassment from dissatisfied clients, competitors, or random "haters." There is a new level of transparency — and thus vulnerability — for even small businesses today. Businesses and even yoga teachers need to have strategies and methods for handling dissatisfied clients gracefully and openly.

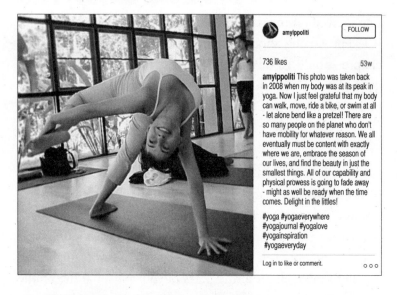

amyippoliti [FOLLOW]

736 likes   53w

amyippoliti This photo was taken back in 2008 when my body was at its peak in yoga. Now I just feel grateful that my body can walk, move, ride a bike, or swim at all - let alone bend like a pretzel! There are so many people on the planet who don't have mobility for whatever reason. We all eventually must be content with exactly where we are, embrace the season of our lives, and find the beauty in just the smallest things. All of our capability and physical prowess is going to fade away - might as well be ready when the time comes. Delight in the littles!

#yoga #yogaeverywhere #yogajournal #yogalove #yogainspiration #yogaeveryday

Log in to like or comment.   ○○○

An Instagram post about my yoga practice that garnered a lot of engagement among my followers. Posts that share personal details tend to receive more engagement than less personal posts.

RESPONDING TO HATERS

If you discover that someone has posted a negative comment about you or your teaching on a social media platform, here's an approach for responding to and defusing it professionally.

1. *Acknowledge* the commenter's point as important and welcomed. Be gracious.
2. *Respond* to the comment. If the person has misunderstood or misrepresented your position on something, politely correct the error. If the comment makes a valid point, acknowledge it and apologize if necessary. If you feel that

there is a genuine difference of opinion, or you don't want to prolong an argument, you may suggest that you both agree to disagree.

3. *Wish the commenter well.* Be kind and friendly as you close your reply. Resist the temptation to tell the person off or say something like, "If you don't like what I post, then unfollow me!" To me, that approach is dismissive rather than engaging and does not embrace this person's right to speak and be heard. A calm, centered, and peace-loving reply will win you the support of other readers, whereas a lashing out or a rebuttal would inevitably result in unfollowers.

A student who came to a retreat with me had this printed on her T-shirt: "May your life someday be as awesome as you pretend it is on Facebook." I had to stop the class to read it and laugh.

Deciding what to share and how to present it on social media platforms can be tricky. It's easy to portray an "awesome" life, and, as the T-shirt slogan suggests, there's a lot of pressure to show that your life is just as awesome as everyone else's. But in addition to not being honest, being relentlessly upbeat and self-promotional doesn't foster genuine connection. (Nor does a self-absorbed oversharing of personal details.) Be yourself.

Although many people choose not to disclose personal details in social media profiles, I believe in using my own name and using a close headshot as my profile picture. Transparency isn't difficult when we aren't pretending.

Overall, always strive to be genuine — about who you are, what you offer, and why you do what you do. And remember that you need never share or reveal more than you are comfortable with. You can't go wrong with these guidelines as your foundation.

CHAPTER EIGHT

Forming Good Professional Relationships

As yoga teachers, we are in a relationship business. To be successful, we must embrace relationship building on many different levels. It's especially important for us to see our students not as devotees who should serve their teacher or guru but as paying clients deserving of nurturing care and attention.

There are seven primary kinds of relationships that are important to yoga teaching:

1. Relationship with the divine
2. Relationship with oneself
3. Relationships with family and friends
4. Relationships with individual students
5. Relationships with staff and colleagues
6. Online relationships
7. Relationships with classes and community

For your own personal growth and for the good of your teaching, it's important to assess each of these types of relationships in your life and ask yourself whether any of them need more attention. This may seem repetitive, but self-inquiry and growth are a huge part of being a yogin.

Let's consider some of these relationships in more detail.

Relationship with the Divine

When we are connected to the divine, we feel more inspired, and thus we teach at our best. But this relationship often gets put on hold when we get busy. Today, with all the distractions of electronic devices and social media, it has become more and more challenging to unplug and find a moment of quiet. When I feel cut off from spirit, I increase my meditation and mantra repetition, get outside, put my bare feet in the grass, light a candle, or write in a gratitude journal. It does not take much to revive the dialogue.

Relationship with Oneself

Yoga teachers are taught to model self-care, but they're often not consistent about following through. Being more stressed than your students is not a basis for good teaching. One of our graduates reported that after she consciously increased her self-care and spent more time unplugged, her teaching improved dramatically. Her students noticed and responded very positively to the difference. We look at self-care at greater length in chapter 13.

Relationships with Family and Friends

According to the author and actor Ben Stein, "Personal relationships are the fertile soil from which all advancement, all success, all achievement in real life grows." Your closest friends, loved ones, and family are vital to your growth and ability to stay inspired as a yoga teacher. When these relationships are nurtured, you also model the importance of personal relationships to your students.

To make sure you're devoting time to tending these relationships, schedule a regular date night with your partner, put regular hang-out time with your kids on your calendar, keep in touch with out-of-town family more consistently, or set up frequent get-togethers with friends.

Relationships with Individual Students

Early in my career, back in 1998, I taught a weekly class in a basement room to sixty-five wholehearted New Yorkers at Crunch Fitness in Manhattan. Little did I know that the relationships I formed in that gym would lead to meaningful lifelong connections.

Every week, I came to class early and stayed after to talk with students, work on their therapeutic issues and injuries, answer their questions — and just hang out and gab. Some people sat around talking for an hour afterward. Most nights after class I brought students with me upstairs to Jivamukti Yoga Center to catch the tail end of Krishna Das's weekly New York kirtans. We'd sing and sway, do *puja*, and delight in the fruit salad prasad.

I am still in touch with many students from that time. Some of them went on to travel with me to new and beautiful places on retreat, and some became master yoga instructors in their own right.

These kinds of students can become loyal supporters who spread the word about your classes and help build a loving community of people around a common interest: yoga.

Relationships with Staff and Colleagues

Do you make a habit of being kind and speaking respectfully to gym and studio staff? I don't claim to be any kind of saint, but I do my best to be friendly and considerate to these colleagues. Not only is this important to my sense of myself, but it makes for easier and more collegial working relationships, which make for better teaching.

Stories abound of yoga teachers at fitness gyms who act entitled, elitist, and pretentious, brusquely demanding specific conditions for their classes and acting as if the other gym staff are ignorant about yoga in general. How much cooperation do you think these teachers are likely to receive?

Because yogins often practice in community, we have a tendency to develop what I call yoga tunnel vision. Yoga, like anything else, can be taken to fanatical levels, to the point where practitioners can't relate to non-yogins! And isn't yoga supposed to be about connection?

Good manners, curiosity, kindness, helpfulness, generosity, enthusiasm, and sensitivity go a long way to demonstrate the spiritual and emotional benefits of yoga, as well as the physical ones, and help yoga continue to grow in the mainstream. Here are some specific ways to nurture relationships with colleagues at a gym or studio.

- *Get to know other teachers at the gym or studio and take their classes.* Learning from other yoga teachers is a vital part of a yoga practice. Taking fitness classes at the gym can boost other aspects of your physical health as well as help you develop good relationships with the other instructors.
- *Attend all meetings and social functions of the gym or studio.* Showing up for meetings and gatherings where

you work, even if you are busy, does two very important things: it helps you know and be a part of the team, and it increases your visibility among managers and students. Managers who see you getting involved with the gym or studio are more likely to give your name when a student asks what class to take or is looking for a teacher to work at a special function, like a wedding party. Attending studio functions lets you get to know current students and gets your name out among potential new students.

- *Keep lines of communication open with colleagues and staff.* Whether you're a studio owner/manager or an employee, touch base regularly with the people you work alongside. Share your needs, goals, visions, feedback, and even grievances. Don't let ill feeling fester to the point where neither party is willing to try to resolve a problem.

- *Maintain good communication by establishing it* before *there's a problem.* If you teach at a studio, for example, chat with the studio owners about getting classes covered, or share with them how you handled a difficult student. By establishing a dialogue when nothing is wrong, you will have a good channel of communication in place if you need to bring up a touchy subject.

- *Be friendly with teachers of other styles of yoga.* It's simply unattractive when a yoga teacher says something negative about another teacher or style of yoga. Don't do it. You're the one who ends up looking bad. Instead, use differences in opinion as an opportunity to see and learn from another perspective.

- *When you don't like something, offer a solution.* If you

are upset about something going on where you work, go directly to the source or the person in charge, state the problem, and then offer to find a solution. This way you won't be seen as a gossiper or complainer.

- *Be a "go-giver," not a "go-getter."* A go-getter comes in, teaches a class, and leaves. A go-giver comes in, sees what they can do to pitch in, and asks what announcements need to be made for upcoming events. After class, they fold blankets, put away props, blow out candles, and pick up water bottles and Kleenex left behind.

  Never think that you are above these tasks. Making this effort increases the feeling of goodwill in the studio, and studio managers who see you pitching in will be more apt to give you prime teaching slots when they open up.

- *Be gracious and show gratitude toward those who have hired you.* Graciousness and gratitude (when you are being paid) is a rare art form these days. The yoga studios and online platforms we talk to complain of yoga teachers behaving as though the world owes them a living, instead of expressing thanks for the opportunity to teach and be paid. Even if you are disappointed with your compensation, expressing thanks for an opportunity goes a very long way toward your being asked back, given a raise, or offered more teaching opportunities, so begin there.

CHAPTER NINE

Managing Your Business Finances

Whether we like it or not, dealing with finances is an inevitable part of working as a yoga teacher. Fortunately, we can learn to do it in ways that reflect our values and visions. We can manage the financial aspects of our business well so that we can pay our bills, live our lives without worry, and build a successful business that enables us to share yoga's benefits and live according to our beliefs and values.

Being stressed out about money will affect your teaching, consciously or unconsciously. Money troubles can make you unfocused and stressed, worrying about how many students are in the room instead of quality teaching. Taking on more classes than you can easily manage in order to make ends meet can make you scattered and unorganized in the classroom. Finally, fretting about money robs teaching of its joy, and your self-esteem will suffer if you come to believe it's impossible for you to make a living.

This chapter takes you through a number of strategies for managing your business finances. You may feel you cannot afford to spend time or money on these financial services or tasks. However, we have found that most yoga teachers who are doing well invested in their future by having a sound financial system in place before they began making substantial money. Let's start with the basics.

- *Create a financial team.* This ideally includes a bookkeeper, an accountant, and/or a financial adviser.
- *Set up a business entity.* Although you can teach yoga and accept payment under your own name, your personal financial situation and your long-term business plans may make it advisable to create a separate business entity. In the United States, you have several options for doing so, and an experienced tax adviser or accountant can help you decide which would be best.
- *Create a bank account just for your yoga teaching and business.* Many yoga teachers simply put the money they make from teaching into a personal account, but if you are going to honor your teaching and take your business seriously, it is important to have clear boundaries. One way to do this is by having a separate account for your business. Talk to your financial advisers about the best way to set up the account.
- *Pay yourself first!* From all my business reading and the many conversations I've had with health and wellness entrepreneurs, it is clear that most successful people pay themselves first. This doesn't necessarily mean literally cutting yourself a paycheck: it means treating a designated portion of your business income as fair payment for your own hard work. Of course, if you run a studio or hire other staff, you need to budget for rent, wages, and other expenses, but this doesn't mean that you should underpay yourself.

• *Save a little every month.* A key part of paying yourself first is investing in yourself by saving. Seeing money grow in a savings or investment account is very rewarding. As your money increases, so does your confidence! The best way to get into the habit of saving is to set up automatic payments into your savings account.

As a starting point, I suggest putting at least 10 percent of your teaching income into savings. This may seem like a daunting amount to set aside when you have bills to pay. But, again, this is a strategy used by many successful teachers and leaders, even when they were first starting out. I have found that once you've put money aside for yourself, you always find a way to earn the amount you need to cover the bills. All the practices outlined in this book are designed to help you increase your earnings, so have faith in yourself!

Insurance

Yoga teachers need two kinds of insurance: health insurance for themselves and their dependents, and liability insurance to protect them against any mishaps that may occur in classes.

Health Insurance

If you live in a country where health care is subsidized and you are already covered, count your blessings and skip ahead! If you live in the United States, read on.

I was shocked to learn how many yoga teachers do not have health insurance in the United States because they feel they cannot afford the monthly premiums. Practicing yoga and living a healthy lifestyle may help ward off illness, but there are no guarantees. At the risk of sounding like a mom, what would you do if you got into a car accident and couldn't pay your hospital bills? Have you ever seen announcements for medical fundraisers in the yoga community? These are typically held to raise funds for a yoga teacher who could not afford medical bills because they did not have health insurance.

Depending on where you live in the United States, you may be able to find a health insurance plan with affordable premiums through the Affordable Care Act ("Obamacare"). If money is really tight, get a policy that covers you just for catastrophic health events. You'll find a way to pay the premium.

If you already have health insurance, make sure you fully understand the kind of policy you have and double-check exactly what you are covered for. For example, a friend of mine, a personal trainer, had a snowmobile crash. His hospital stay cost a fortune. Although his health insurance policy offered comprehensive benefits, he had failed to notice that it did not cover this kind of incident. Because his work, like teaching yoga, was hands-on and physical, he could not return to work to pay the bills. He lost everything. Don't place yourself at this kind of risk: put the money aside for a health insurance policy and read all the fine print.

Liability Insurance

Most of us don't want to believe that our students would ever be litigious, and in truth, most students are not. Moreover, when properly taught, yoga is a very safe form of physical activity. Occasionally, however, yoga teachers face liability lawsuits. In 2009, a student sued a prominent yoga studio in Boulder, Colorado. The student claimed that he had been permanently injured by a hands-on assist given by one of the teachers. The studio and teacher were protected from financial disaster by their liability insurance. Paying for liability insurance is very inexpensive compared to unconsciously worrying about injuries every time you teach or having a potentially devastating lawsuit hanging over you.

Business liability insurance is available from various sources. Yoga Journal works with a great insurance company to provide a liability policy called Yoga Journal Teachers (Plus) that costs, as I write, under $200 a year.

LIABILITY RELEASES

Yoga studios generally require all new students to sign a liability release form, or waiver. If you are conducting yoga classes outside of an established studio, however, it's your responsibility to have students release you from liability. It's best to consult with an attorney to create a standard liability release you can have students sign to protect you, in addition to carrying your own liability insurance policy.

Contribution and *Seva*

Does the topic of charitable contributions belong in a chapter on business finances? For yoga teachers, yes. Involvement in volunteer work, charity, philanthropy, or *seva* (the Sanskrit word for service) is a huge part of what yoga is about — and, as an added bonus, it inspires your teaching. The beauty of service is that it not only assists the people you are serving but also enhances your self-esteem, and this makes you a better teacher. Here are just a few of the many benefits of being involved in some form of *seva*:

- It teaches humility.
- It inspires and gives your identity as a teacher more meaning.
- It is a great way to build community and connection.
- It gives your teaching more purpose.
- It cultivates abundance and energy, because the universe sees that you are giving back and that you are ready for more.
- It makes you feel uplifted because you feel useful.

Giving back is fundamental to human existence. For most of the last month of my grandmother's life, when she was in hospice, she would hug and give everyone sweet compliments. It was her way of giving back, even though she was weak and in pain. When she reached a point where she could barely talk or wrap her arms around people anymore I saw that she was getting ready to leave. It was as though if she could no longer give back, she was done. She lived only another three days.

Being of service to others helps us feel useful and valued. Having *seva* as part of our lives can be a source of deep motivation and inspiration. It also makes for wonderful anecdotes to share with our students. When we give and we feel of use, not only in our teaching but in other ways too, we can share our feelings of encouragement and inspiration with our students. For more on *seva* and karma yoga, see chapter 14.

Part III

TEACHING WELL

CHAPTER TEN

Class Planning and Preparation

To teach well, we all need a good "container." The Sanskrit word for container is *dharana*. The container holds what you put into it. Having excellent training and being a skilled teacher are important things to put into your container, but solid preparation and organization also need to be in there.

It's easy to understand why students appreciate good preparation. Teachers who are well organized remember what they did in the previous class, continue where they left off, and know and remember the health concerns or challenges of regular students. Their classes flow well, with smooth sequences, helpful cues, and interesting themes and anecdotes. And organization gives the teachers themselves the mental space to plan classes that keep things fresh for them as well as for their students.

Yet in a recent poll of our teacher trainees, Taro and I found that only 22 percent always felt prepared and organized for class. What are the challenges that keep us from preparing well? Here are some suggestions to identify and help overcome them.

Create a Packing List

When teaching in person, create a list of things you'll need for each day's classes, and consult it before you leave home so that you won't forget any important items. My list includes items I need for teaching, such as my class plans or binder, music, bells (to take students out of savasana), and yoga mat and cushion, if needed. Sometimes I remind myself to bring along a handout or small gift for the students too. I also include marketing materials, such as my mailing list sign-up sheet, postcards for upcoming events, and business cards. Making a list might sound trivial; however, there's a reason pilots go through a preflight checklist no matter how often they fly. How many times have you gone to a grocery store to pick up three items, only to return home with ten items and only one of the three you intended to buy?

Keep a Teaching Binder

I love my teaching binder because it helps me keep my teaching fresh and inspired. Your binder is where you can store all your ideas, teaching notes, stick-figure drawings, client notes, theme ideas, and thoughts about yoga philosophy and life in general.

You can create a tool like this either in an old-style three-ring binder or on an electronic device. Either way, it should be in a form you can bring with you and refer to easily in class. I still use a pen and paper because they somehow slow me down and get me back to basics. Even if you're a devoted tablet or computer user, you might try writing by hand once in a while to see if it provokes a different line of thought.

Having a binder keeps all your ideas at your fingertips. On days when you are not feeling inspired, you can open the binder and get an idea for class.

I suggest keeping the following sections in your binder.

Mission Statement

Your mission statement comes first and foremost in your binder (see pages 39–40). In this section you can keep all your brainstorming notes. I can't tell you how many times I have felt dull and uninspired before teaching a class. When I ask myself, "Why am I doing this?" and look at my mission statement, I always get a spark of inspiration and an idea for the class.

Values

Keep the list of values that you came up with earlier (see pages 33–37) in this section so you have it at your fingertips.

REHEARSALS

If you teach a style of yoga in which you typically share more than simple physical instructions — for example, when you are working with a theme or integrating yoga philosophy — what you share has to be genuine, concise, and easy for students to relate to so that it doesn't come across as pretentious or hokey. If you rehearse what you plan to say to a friend or significant other before class and accept feedback, it will come across much more effectively and genuinely.

Contemplations and Anecdotes

One of the things that makes a yoga class different from a fitness class is that it often includes an inspirational message given at the beginning of or during class. Students often enjoy hearing teachers' personal stories or their takes on subjects such as the *yamas* and *niyamas*, the *gunas*, or the *koshas*. It's critical, though, to keep these messages succinct, sincere, and focused, or they'll irritate students instead of inspiring them. Regularly write down the insights and metaphors that occur to you and collect them in your binder. Consulting this treasure trove before or during class can help you frame an effective message that's uniquely yours.

Themes

In this section you can keep an ongoing list of ideas for class themes (see pages 188–96 for details). Browsing the list is a great way to come up with an idea for your next class.

Class Plans

Keeping your class plans all in one place gives you flexibility: you can reuse a class plan on a day when you don't have time to plan anything new, or reuse a successful plan with a different group of students. The more you plan your classes, the more plans you'll have to draw on for future use. See my example of a class planning template later in this chapter.

Keeping a library of plans also serves as a great record of what you have done previously with your students. It's also a good place to note sequences you enjoyed while taking classes from other teachers.

If you are auditioning to teach somewhere new, or anytime

you are nervous, use your favorite plans (the classes where you knocked it out of the park) to boost your confidence and offer your best teaching.

REPETITION IS THE MOTHER OF LEARNING

Some teachers feel they are cheating or lazy if they repeat a class plan. While it's important to be fresh and do different things with your students, a certain amount of repetition is appropriate. In fact, many students love repetition and the chance to improve on something they have done before. Yoga is a *practice*, after all!

Instruction Notes

Knowing your poses and demonstrating them perfectly is not the same thing as being able to explain them clearly to students during class when you are not in the pose. If you write up your cues and instructions, you can work through them and rehearse them before class. After class, you can come back and write down the instructions that worked best for students.

If you teach vinyasa yoga and are new to teaching, this can be a place to get clear on inhale versus exhale instructions. When I first had to teach a sun salutation, I could not remember how to connect the elements of the sequence to inhalation and exhalation. So I wrote out my cues for the sequence of a sun salutation word for word and practiced with a tape recorder before I taught.

If you use technical instructions or cues based on anatomical alignment, or if you tend to confuse left and right, working the cues out on paper helps you say them clearly and precisely. Teachers who can provide succinct instructions to help their students get into the correct poses provide a much smoother class experience.

DO THE TWIST

The instructions for getting students into a simple twist like ardha matsyendrasana can be very complex. To illustrate this point, compare these two sets of placement instructions.

1. "Okay. What we're going to do now is cross your right leg over the left knee and place that foot on the ground. Then bend that left knee so your foot sits by your hip — I mean the right hip. Sit up tall, and then twist to your right, placing your right hand on the ground behind you and wedging your left elbow against the left-hand side of your left knee — oh, wait, I meant the right knee. Inhaling, straighten your spine, and exhaling, twist to your right and look to the right."

2. "Cross your right foot over your left knee and place it on the floor. Bend your left leg and draw the heel toward your right hip. Hook your left elbow to the outside of your right knee and place your right hand behind you. As you inhale, get tall. As you exhale, twist to the right and look over your right shoulder."

Which one did you understand better? The second one was written out ahead of time and is clear, short, and succinct.

Vinyasa Flows

A variety of mini-vinyasa flows (shorter sequences within the overall class sequence) helps keep classes interesting. Anyone can come up with new sequences using a sticky mat as a laboratory. Trying them out first instead of inventing them on the fly in class will allow you to make sure that they're accessible and graceful before springing them on your students.

Creative mini-vinyasas are like gold! Write them down and file them in this section.

Quotes

Keep a section of your favorite quotations by famous authors, teachers, and artists and use them to support your class themes and inspire your students with something more than just stretching.

You can also file quotes according to topic, such as self-love, getting through difficult times, seeing the silver lining, empowerment, and mindfulness. Then if you are teaching a class on any of these themes, you can easily find appropriate quotes to use in class.

Student and Client Notes

Keep a record of your clients' achievements, challenges, and poses done in class. This is useful for group classes, but it's especially good for private clients, because usually more time passes between private sessions, and it's easy to forget what you covered in the previous session.

Useful Verbs

All yoga cues use verbs, both literal and metaphorical. Words and phrases like *extend, root, ground, draw in, reach out,* and *melt* are used to describe movement in yoga.

It's easy to fall into a stale pattern of repeating the same verbs over and over. Keep a list of good alternatives for describing poses and sequences, drawn from your reading, other classes and activities, and even the thesaurus.

Four categories of verbs are particularly relevant to yoga sequences. Here are some you can use to give students a richer experience.

> *General:* Words and phrases like *ground, extend, expand, inflate, widen, tap into, attract.*
>
> *Hydraulic:* When you are teaching a class that has a theme relating to the water element, you can use verbs such as *pour, stream,* and *flow.*
>
> *Photic:* For any class theme that has to do with light — finding your inner light, finding the light at the end of the tunnel, or being a brighter light in the world — consider using verbs such as *shine, beam, radiate, blaze, glow,* and *sparkle.*
>
> *Sonic:* In a class with a theme related to vibration or pulsation, use verbs related to sound, such as *echo, resonate,* and *reverberate.*

How Much Should You Plan?

How structured should your classes be? Should you adhere to a rigid class plan or suit your sequences to your own state of mind, the vibe among the students in the room, or sudden inspiration? Here are issues to consider on both sides.

Pros of Planning

Planning is calming and gives you confidence, especially when you are starting out. The process helps you get to know your material, thus increasing the capacity of your *dharana*! Students appreciate that you have taken the time to think about the class beforehand. And even if you want to take a more fluid and improvisational approach in class, it helps to have a backup plan. It can give you the confidence to experiment, knowing that if inspiration fails, you can always return to the plan.

Cons of Planning

Sticking too closely to a class plan can make your teaching overly rigid and can make it harder for you to be present to the students in the room and what is needed in the moment. It can close you off from other possibilities and make you unspontaneous.

There are ways to strike a balance between rigid planning and chaos. Although I recommend that you always have some kind of plan, I also think that good, deep preparation for teaching should enable you to depart from that plan when the occasion arises. As you teach, pay attention to what's happening in the room rather than always adhering to your plan.

Be confident in your teaching. The fact that you have invested the time and thought to plan a class means that you have all the skills and knowledge in your head to teach without notes.

Use a Class Planning Template

Using a template to plan allows you to consider all the elements of your yoga class beforehand, including your theme, your sequence of poses, hands-on assists you want to offer, music you might want to play, and how to pace the class.

Once you have planned about twenty classes using a template, you'll have a valuable repertoire of class plans that you can reuse or adapt. This can be especially useful if you're short on time to

VINYASA PLANNING TEMPLATE

NIMESHA/CIT
Contractive

MADHYA
Spanda

UNMESHA/ANANDA
Expansive

ANECDOTES

PHYSICAL FOCUS

PHILOSOPHICAL FOCUS

plan a class or if you have to change a plan on the fly to meet the specific needs of the students who showed up. Even after all my years of teaching, I still use my class planning templates.

The template shown here (adjusted slightly to fit the pages of this book) is the result of years of scribbling down sequences, contemplations, and pacing notes for my classes. I wanted a structure that would let me write down all the elements of a good yoga class. After working on a number of iterations, I presented

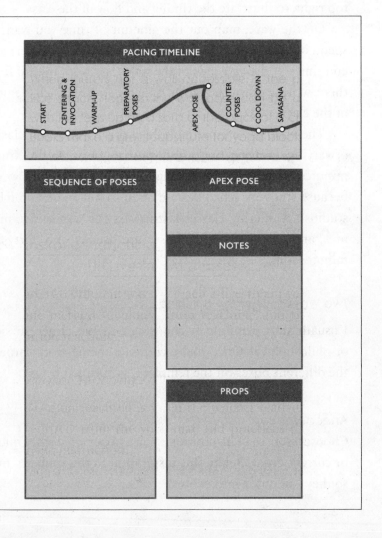

my design to a graphic artist, who came up with the template I still use today. You can use it as a model to create your own template, or find a downloadable version at Vesselify.com.

Visual Aids: Bird and Wave Graphics

The template includes two visual elements: the bird at the top left, to map the dynamics of the class theme, a quick-reference snapshot of your overall theme; and the wave at the top right, to illustrate the timing and flow of the class.

On the wave, map out the amount of time you want to spend on each element of the class. Mark the class's start and end times at the two ends of the wave, and work inward from there, writing down the target time for starting each element of the class.

The wave can be particularly useful if you teach classes of varying duration, as you will probably have to do. Ninety minutes is the traditional length of a yoga class. However, because students' schedules are often so full, more and more studios are offering classes lasting sixty to seventy-five minutes, and corporate yoga classes are usually only forty-five minutes long.

Two Ways to Start the Planning Process

I usually start planning by choosing a theme, either physical or philosophical. Once you've chosen a theme, work through the different boxes on the template, as outlined below.

Anecdotes Box

Choose a source of inspiration, such as a personal story, quote, or current event. Relate this inspiration to the students' lives so they can put it into context.

Physical Focus Box

Reflect on what key physical actions you want to focus on, such as those required for the apex pose (if any) or how the physical actions of the class relate to the philosophical theme.

Philosophical Focus Box

If I'm using a philosophical theme, I ask myself what the philosophical message of the class will be. There's more information on themes later in this chapter.

Sequence of Poses Box

Write out your full class sequence of poses.

Apex Pose Box

Choose an apex pose that corresponds to the physical actions and philosophical theme. It should be the most challenging pose in the sequence and appropriate for most of the students in the class. (This step is optional, as you can teach a perfectly great class that never peaks to a particular pose.)

Notes Box

Use this box to jot down any thoughts and ideas about any aspects of the class before you organize them into the template. You can also use this box to anticipate what hands-on assists you want to give. Of course, you can also do this on a separate sheet of paper.

Props Box

You guessed it, use this box to anticipate what props you might need to enhance and personalize the poses in your sequence so that when students ask, you're ready with a clear answer on what props they can gather before class.

STANDARD SEQUENCING ELEMENTS
OF AN ASANA CLASS

Every teacher has a slightly different take on sequencing, but in general you want to include and time the following elements:

Centering: Centering helps students transition to the practice from their busy days.

Warm-up: A warm-up eases students into their bodies before they perform any challenging poses.

Standing poses: Standing poses work well in the first half of class because they warm up the body so effectively. They are a classic way to teach alignment techniques and build stamina and confidence.

Abdominals or core work: Engaging the core happens naturally throughout the practice; however, it can be useful to teach specific core or "ab" work to prepare and strengthen the body for the increased range of motion and flexibility required for most bendy yoga poses.

Inversions and arm balances: Like core work and standing poses, inversions and arm balances demand stamina, build heat, and engage the core, so they are great for strengthening the body before moving on to poses that demand flexibility.

Preparatory poses: Before attempting more advanced or apex poses, lead students through a series of poses to warm up and target the specific body parts involved.

Apex/pinnacle pose or more challenging asanas: Using the wave, budget enough time for students to experiment and play with the apex pose or the grouping of challenging asanas.

Counterposes: After the apex pose or set of challenging asanas, it's time to teach a series of counterposes that counteracts the movements performed during the peak of the class.

Cool-down/seated poses: As part of the cool-down period, it's nice to add seated poses, such as hip openers and forward bends, before going into the stillness of savasana.

Meditation: You may choose to add a brief meditation period in which students can sit, close their eyes, and take in and feel the practice in silence.

Savasana (final relaxation): Working backward from the tail end of the wave, you can choose how long savasana will last, so you know when your cool-down and seated poses should end. Typically, savasana is three to ten minutes long, depending on the duration of the class.

You can use the same class plan more than once in the same week or use it for an entire week, depending on who shows up. Even if a few students attend the repeated classes, you will usually teach them slightly differently, according to your mood and the needs of the students. And you often teach a class better the second or third time through.

Using Themes

One of the biggest questions that comes up in our training classes is whether and how to use themes. Giving a class a specific theme helps you distinguish yoga from mere stretching and creates a richer experience on the mat.

If you keep a journal, either on paper or digitally, a great way to generate ideas for themes and anecdotes is to write frequently about how various events in your life relate to yoga and vice versa. If you don't keep a journal, consider carrying a small notebook or creating a digital notepad for this kind of brainstorming.

To use these insights as class themes, you'll need to express them in a way that students can understand and relate to. Even a person who has never heard of the Eight Limbs or the word *Om* should be able to understand what you mean. Ask yourself what makes your insight or theme relevant to everyone in the room.

Telling personal stories can help you relate to your students and get off the teacher's pedestal. But keep them short, especially if the students are sitting in positions that may become uncomfortable and they are anxious to move. Do your best not to focus too much on yourself or your life: not everyone wants to hear a story about your wise and adorable kids in every class. And avoid being self-aggrandizing. It's nice to tell a story in which you learn something, but not one that makes you sound like you're now the most enlightened person on the planet.

Know Why Your Theme Matters

When considering a theme, ask yourself: So what? Why is this relevant and important? Why should anyone care?

It's great if you can link a physical activity theme to a philosophical purpose. For example, when teaching a class with a hip opening emphasis, you might tell your students that opening the hips can be beneficial during difficult times. You might start by saying that hip opening helps you get grounded. But why is getting grounded important? You might explain that being grounded imparts a sense of settled calm to those around you. And why is that important? You might answer that when people around us are settled, they will be living with more kindness and awareness, resulting in more harmony throughout the whole world.

I once took a class in a rural area with an older, experienced teacher who had a strong student base and a very full classroom. At first I really wasn't sure why she was so well respected. However, when she stopped to do an appropriate and succinct demonstration of tree pose for some elderly beginner students in the room, she spoke about how creating strength in the supporting leg would help the students be pillars of strength for their loved ones. Instantly the energy in the room increased, the students' faces lit up, and the remainder of the class was much more captivating and engaging.

Connecting yoga to its highest purpose, even just once per class, can make a huge difference. Here are some categories of themes that can help you do that.

Pulsation-Based Themes

Pulsation (*spanda* in Sanskrit) is reflected everywhere in nature — in the tides coming in and receding, day and night, life and death, light and dark, and so on. In our bodies, we have oppositions like front and back, open and closed, left and right. You can incorporate these ideas into a class theme, encouraging students to find the sweet spot between opposites, which is often a gateway for deeper opening. When you balance the front and back of the body when performing a pose, you usually unfold with more ease. Examples of this type of theme include the following:

- Effort/surrender
- Masculine/feminine
- Courage/contentment
- Intention and desire / letting go

Natural Cycles

Students easily relate to season changes, solstices and equinoxes, and moon cycles, since these are part of our shared experience. Many are starved for nature, so themes like this offer a way to integrate nature into a class and contemplate how we can be inspired by the natural world and its changes.

Yoga Philosophy

If you have a student audience that is open to traditional yoga teachings, you can use lectures or seminars you've attended on yoga philosophy as a great source of themes. The teachings in the texts are infinite: pick something that you and your students can particularly relate to.

Another source of inspiration is the Hindu pantheon of gods and goddesses. Each one, with their particular personal attributes and lessons, can provide a theme.

Insights from Your Yoga Practice and Personal Development

Insights and "aha" moments from your own practice and life may be more motivating and exciting to your students than you think — share them! They make wonderful themes. Students enjoy knowing what you are working on and joining in the challenge. For example, you might tell your students, "This month I am focusing on trust and honesty," and invite them to share in that contemplation. Offer a statement of your focus that's catchy and easy to remember, such as "Trust and be true." Some core messages I have heard include the following:

- Gratitude
- Respect
- Letting go of complaining, blaming, justifying, or excuses
- Being open to infinite source and abundance
- Self-compassion
- Living from the heart
- Getting back to the basics

Postural Themes

Postural themes — for example, a focus on the breath, standing poses, shoulders, hips, or endurance — might seem purely physical; however, if you dig deep enough, you'll find they are also meaningful and philosophical. For example, the breath is the link between the physical and the divine. Standing poses engender empowerment and help us cultivate confidence and steadfast remembrance. And the shoulders are connected to the heart center, where we experience vulnerability and love.

The Chakras

The chakras are a rich source of themes, as they represent how we relate to ourselves as well as to the world around us.

For example, the root chakra, which is seated in the pelvic floor, has to do with feeling grounded and safe. A whole class can be structured around those qualities while focusing on opening the hips.

Inspiration from the Apex Pose

If your class is structured to build to an apex pose, chances are that this peak pose has a story or an interesting name, or it challenges and opens the body in an enriching and empowering way. For example, ardha chandrasana (half-moon pose), a fairly basic peak pose, has a lot of character! With arms and legs extended, it gives a feeling of flying and freedom, and the supporting leg expresses confidence and stability.

Books, Art, and Movies

Books, art exhibitions, and movies keep you current, inspired, and creative and often supply excellent themes. So do inspiring talks and other cultural events in your community. Students enjoy having their yoga practice come together with something off the mat. After watching *The Wizard of Oz* a few years ago, I was moved by how each character in the story was on their own quest for something they felt they needed in order to be whole. For Dorothy it was finding her way home; for the Scarecrow it was getting a brain; for the Tin Man it was receiving a heart; and for the Lion it was finding courage. Although they started out believing that the Wizard could give them what they sought, they learned that the Wizard was just a little man behind the curtain, and they realized that everything they were seeking was already inside them. Sounds a lot like yoga, right? You can probably imagine the relatable class themes that came out of seeing that movie again!

Celebrations

You can choose a theme related to world or national holidays or a famous person's birthday. Holidays are easy to find using Google, and almost every day is a holiday somewhere in the world! The history of a holiday, as well as the associated traditions, ceremonies, and celebrations, can be of interest. You can also plan a class around a student's birthday, honoring the positive qualities of that person and structuring the practice to cultivate those qualities.

Here in the United States, Valentine's Day and Thanksgiving are two of my favorite holidays. Since Valentine's Day is about love and Thanksgiving is about gratitude, you can't go wrong using them as class themes.

One Valentine's Day, I lined the walkway to the studio with rose petals and lit the room with dozens of soy tea lights. I played schmaltzy, romantic ballads from the seventies and eighties as students entered the studio. I put organic chocolate hearts on everyone's mat during savasana. Realizing that romantic love might be a sensitive or painful theme for some students, I focused the practice on cultivating self-love and allowing relationships to be the "cherry on top" of an already meaningful life.

Chance Inspiration

You never know what might get you and your students fired up. It could be a slogan you saw on a billboard. It could be song lyrics that move you. It could be your children and the deep, funny, and truthful things they say. Be open to inspiration as you go through your day.

Current Events

Current events can affect everyone, and acknowledging them can be very powerful. Whether it is a climate-related disaster, a community tragedy, or the Olympics, integrating current events into your class themes can deepen the practice. For more on this, see chapter 14, "Leadership and Karma Yoga (Regenerative Practices and Social Change)."

Life Challenges

Everyone experiences personal tragedy and crisis at some time. You can make these experiences into valuable class themes, showing your students what you learned and who you are now because of them.

I used to think that I couldn't teach while I dealt with personal life challenges. But after trying both subbing out my classes and teaching through the difficult times, I've found that I'm much happier showing up for class and integrating the challenge into my teaching than taking a break.

In the month following the attacks on the World Trade Center in New York City on September 11, 2001, I felt vulnerable and fragile as I attempted to pull myself together to teach. The Wall Street gym where I worked was inaccessible, and most of my students there had been directly affected by the attacks.

When I was able to teach again, I tried to acknowledge the pain everyone felt and uplift them in the face of such madness. It was intense and difficult. At the end of the day, in my apartment, I would fall onto the floor and cry. Yet this experience helped me learn to integrate grieving with teaching. Years later, when I went through a devastating divorce, I didn't miss a class and my teaching felt stronger than ever.

TURNING DIFFICULTY INTO OPPORTUNITY

Yoga is the process of skillfully turning challenges, failures, hurts, and mistakes into opportunities.

Experiencing sadness and pain can offer us insight into how to soothe others in need. The challenges I've lived through fuel my fire to teach others to apply yoga to their lives. I let each of the betrayals, hurts, losses, and crimes light me on fire, then I set every yoga mat in the room on fire (metaphorically speaking, of course!).

If you have lost a loved one, you might dedicate the class to that person's specific virtues and acknowledge how every life leaves blessings for us all. Use the opportunity to explore the idea of living fully now, and guide students to consider the legacy they might want to leave behind.

If you have been betrayed, consider how yoga philosophy and deeper self-awareness could be applied to help you respond positively in the face of betrayal. Teach a class focusing on the virtues of truth, friendship, integrity, and making life-affirming choices.

If you are going through a crisis and have a full teaching schedule, teach that the only constant in life is change, and that crisis always brings opportunity. Remember, though, when you're teaching, yoga class is not about you. Take time in private to cry, grieve, and fully feel your experience. Make very sure you have an outlet for anger, disappointment, and hurt so that your students never have to be your therapists. Reach out to peers, counselors, and your teachers for support. When crisis is acute and you are simply too raw to teach, by all means stay home and get your classes covered until you're confident in front of others. Once that happens, even if you are still healing, keep your teaching focused on other things. Otherwise you set your students up to have to take care of you, when during class you should be the one caring for them.

If you do share any part of your crisis, make sure that you're doing it after already having come to some resolution about the crisis, so that you can inspire others to have faith when they are going through difficulty.

GOING THEME-FREE

If you can't focus on a theme and connect it to what you're doing throughout the class, skip it! Classes with no theme can be spacious and allow students to simply practice. I've also seen classes work well where the theme is stated only once at the beginning and not mentioned again, giving students a moment to contemplate a teaching and then letting them apply it in their own way throughout the practice, with no reminder from the teacher. The key with themes is to be aware of what approach you are taking and maintain it.

With the help of your yoga binder, your class plan, and openness to inspiration for class themes, you'll be ready to offer your very best teaching to your students every time you teach a class.

CHAPTER ELEVEN

Teaching In-Person Classes Skillfully

When you deliver a well-thought-out, safe, and inspiring class experience, students will want to return again and again. If your teaching truly inspires them, they may move toward living a lifestyle whose wellspring is yoga, which benefits everyone around them.

Open Up to Receive Divine Direction

If you've had the chance to watch an extremely talented musician perform, it often seems as though some other presence is within them, making their hands play the instrument. The divine pours through them. That power can bring audiences to their feet in a spontaneous standing ovation. We have all experienced the divine to some degree when we are performing, working out, playing sports, dancing, or on the yoga mat: it's the feeling of being "in the zone."

When Michael Jackson passed away, I, like many other people, avidly watched Michael Jackson videos on YouTube. (Although the abuse allegations against Michael Jackson are to be taken seriously, his talent was unmistakable and we can learn things from his gifts as an artist.) I came across an intimate interview with him. The interviewer asked Jackson, "How do you come up with these things, like where did you come up with that beat in 'Billie Jean'? How is this possible?" Jackson paused and answered, "That's the thing. It did not come from me, that came from up above! Artists have to get out of their own way." This is true for yoga teachers too. When we think too much, we get in our own way and lose the chance to be assisted and inspired by something bigger.

Before you begin teaching, give yourself time to get into a state that allows the divine to pour through you. The students will feel the difference and be moved by the clarity of your offering. Even if your schedule is crowded, try to leave time for a few minutes alone before class to get yourself centered.

WAYS TO BECOME A VESSEL FOR THE DIVINE

Sit with your intention to be a vessel. Meditate on it in whatever way works for you. I close my eyes and concentrate on my breath.

I have found it helpful to do an inversion before class and to chant a beautiful *Om*.

Focusing on your mission as a teacher, do a ritual or prayer before class, recite mantras in all corners of the room, and give yourself a bit of practice time before class. When I teach pranayama in the beginning of the class, I find it helpful to do the practice with the students when possible.

Parcel It Out

Another incredible talent of Michael Jackson was his ability to tease his audience. He would hold himself back just enough to drive them crazy. He'd restrain his vocals, hold a silent moment for a painfully long time, or restrict his dance movements to a staccato. He wasn't giving them everything they wanted: he was giving them just enough. Fans in the audience would literally pass out from anticipation.

You also see this phenomenon in performances by the best kirtan musicians. Krishna Das, known as the King of Kirtan, is my favorite example. For years he has built his chants slowly and gradually, riding the back of the beat, never letting it play too fast. He'll cast sideways glances at the other musicians and bell players when they start to push the rhythm too quickly. When he finally speeds up, the whole room explodes! People stand up, start dancing, throw their arms in the air, and clap wildly.

You don't need to pull any crazy dance moves in your yoga class or imitate a kirtan singer. Teaching yoga is not a stage performance, but there is something to be said for adopting some of the pacing and restraint of these star artists.

Many teachers make the mistake of saying too much, speaking without ever pausing and giving more information than students can absorb in one class rather than parceling it out in bits and pieces. If you give your students just enough, they will be hungry for more of what you have to offer, both in your group classes and in your other more in-depth offerings. One mistake is trying to cram the content of a three-hour workshop into a sixty-minute class. Students may end up sitting around listening to your opening dharma talk and then watching you demonstrate poses while emphasizing a long list of alignment instructions, when they came to class to move.

Don't be in a rush to impart all your knowledge in one class session. Remember, your classes aren't going anywhere, and hopefully your students aren't either. The biggest compliment I ever received while teaching at a hot flow yoga studio (and I do like to teach alignment-based yoga) was something like, "We sweat and flow, but I always glean some little gem from your classes that helps me go deeper in my poses, Amy." I have a lot of gems to share — far too many to count. You do too. The key is to share those gems just a few at a time so that your students want more.

Presence

Presence is that remarkable ability for a teacher to connect with students in such a way that the students are completely absorbed in what the teacher has to say. Cultivating presence is not simply a matter of innate charisma. It involves conscious effort by the teacher: looking students in the eye, observing them carefully, and getting to know them and their needs. Everyone wants to feel "seen" in this way.

Relating Well to Students

There are a number of simple things you can do (and *not* do!) to make students feel seen, included, welcomed, comfortable, and enthusiastic so that they'll keep coming back to your yoga classes. If you're not sure how well your presentation is going down with students, video recording can be helpful, or you might ask a friend to attend one of your classes and give feedback. Of course, you can also ask your students for feedback, using an anonymous paper or online questionnaire.

Below are some positive habits to cultivate and a few not-so-good ones to eliminate.

Positive Teaching Habits

Here are some pointers for leading a smoothly flowing, rewarding forty-five- to ninety-minute class:

- *Speak succinctly.* Put yourself in the position of your students and try to hear yourself from their perspective. You obviously don't want to tell a long story while your students are holding a difficult pose.
- *Explain why what you are saying is valuable.* It is easy to forget to clearly explain to students why a story, anecdote, myth, or traditional teaching is important, especially when its value is obvious to you. How will this information help them? If you can't come up with an answer, skip the speech!
- *Connect personally with students*, making eye contact with them rather than talking over them.
- *Keep initial centering at the start of class short.* Ideally, wrap it up within three minutes and get your students moving. Five minutes should be the max.
- *Start warm-up with a vinyasa* (one pose per inhale/exhale). In evening classes, most students are coming from work. They have likely sat at a desk all day and now are ready to move. Avoid having these students sit for long periods or talking to them too much right at the beginning. A vinyasa will help them get moving and blow off steam.
- *Come to class prepared.* I can't emphasize this point

too strongly. There is nothing worse than a teacher facing a roomful of students and asking, "So, what do you all want to work on tonight? I didn't have time to prepare."

- *State the class theme* clearly at the start of class and reinforce it one to three times during the class.
- *Pause* to allow students to breathe when in poses.
- *Be spacious in your teaching.* Once you have given your best, most succinct points about alignment and philosophy, allow your students to do their practice, and stick to guiding them in that practice rather than talking more. Some will ask for your assistance; others will cherish a quiet opportunity to execute your instructions and feel the results.
- *Know when a demo is necessary.* When I see that students are struggling to understand my instructions, or I'm teaching a pose they have never seen before, I'll gather them around quickly for a demonstration, either doing the pose myself or asking a student to help me demonstrate. The demo lasts no longer than sixty seconds; otherwise, the students will get antsy. I try to time it to come just after the students have done something fairly strenuous, so that a break is welcome.
- *Attend to every student in the class at least once* with a hands-on assist or an acknowledgment. I once put up a question on Facebook asking what people wanted more of in yoga class, and the majority responded that they would like more hands-on assists. Not everyone wants to be touched, though, so ask first. If they say yes, then get to it. For students who do not want to be touched, offer other forms of acknowledgment, such as

making eye contact or addressing them by name. Make a point of giving individual attention to everyone in the room at least once during class. And don't skimp on savasana — give savasana assists as well.

Some of these things will come naturally to you as a teacher, and others may be points you have to work on. It takes a while to reinforce a new habit so that it becomes second nature.

Not-So-Positive Teaching Habits

Here are a few habits that students consistently say they dislike in teachers:

- Talking too much about yourself
- Repeating yourself
- Suggesting that your method of yoga is superior to other methods
- Excessive partner work or demos
- Having "in" jokes with some students
- Departing from the published title or description of the class
- Excessive yoga jargon and clichés

PARTNER WORK

Students who work with people all day or negotiate the needs of family members often do not want to engage in partner work during yoga class. They want their space and a bit of solo time. Some dislike partner work for other reasons, including feeling uncomfortable about touching others or nervous about spotting them. In addition, partner work takes time to explain and arrange and can disrupt the flow of a class. For these reasons, although it may occasionally be useful in sixty-minute to ninety-minute classes, I think it is best reserved for workshops, retreats, or dedicated partner classes.

In longer-format classes and workshops, partner work can be valuable because it allows everyone to receive hands-on assists and spots, enhancing understanding and ability and enabling everyone to advance much faster. To ensure safety, it's important to teach the spot or assist in as much detail as the pose itself. This requires very clear instructions and demonstration, and you'll need to monitor partner work vigilantly to make sure it is being executed properly.

S**T YOGA TEACHERS SAY:
STEREOTYPICAL YOGA SPEAK

We asked our Facebook followers to list phrases they thought sounded canned or inauthentic from yoga teachers. The responses included the following:

- "It's all good"
- "Calm your mind"
- "Just be!"
- "Just relax"
- Anything that starts with the word *just*!
- "Let go of your thoughts"
- "Release your monkey mind"
- "Peel away the layers like an onion"
- "Open your heart"

Of course, many of these phrases have become clichés precisely because they contain valuable truths. The way to make them sound less hackneyed is to make them relevant to the lives of your students or give an example of their potency in your own life.

Cultivating New Habits

If any of this feedback from students has made you think there are teaching habits you should change, then make a list of them. Focus on changing them one at a time. It takes one to three weeks of conscious effort to develop a new habit or break an old one. For example, if you tend to talk too much, use the next two weeks to focus on the skill of speaking more economically, with silent pauses to give students the time to experience their poses.

SELL YOUR SUB

When you have to miss a class, let your students know in advance, and praise the teacher you have lined up as a substitute. Although you might legitimately worry that the students will not show up for the sub, not telling them about your absence is unfair to the students and sets them up to be disappointed and dissatisfied when they arrive for class.

One way to strike a positive, community-oriented note is to introduce your sub as a guest teacher rather than a sub. Let the students know that this teacher is a colleague, tell them all the reasons why the teacher is fabulous, and emphasize that you want your students to keep practicing while you're absent. Tell them you want them to stay strong and in "yoga shape" for the things you have planned on your return.

Work with the other teacher to plan what kind of class to teach and maintain continuity in the students' practice. You can then enthusiastically share your guest teacher's class plans and let them know you will be building on those classes when you return. This kind of cooperation and enthusiasm shows that both you and the guest teacher care about the students and about offering quality teaching.

Handling Multiple Ability Levels in Class

Most yoga teachers lead open or multilevel classes. These can be challenging to teach, because if you don't cater to everyone, attendance can suffer.

I've had beginners walk out in horror the minute I asked everyone to come to the wall to attempt to kick into handstand. I've had advanced students popping into full scorpion pose during forearm balance at the wall because they wanted to go deeper. And I've had a student with a truckload of props to modify poses for an acute injury working right next to a yogin with her leg behind her head.

If you're teaching an open-level class, you are implicitly telling students it is safe and appropriate for them to be there. Through trial and much error, I have come up with a number of strategies to make sure I am serving my students well in multilevel classes.

First, give a disclaimer. Clearly state the nature of the class at the start so that you empower the students to take responsibility for their own energy and well-being and to speak up if they need help. Here are some ways to say it:

- "We have multiple levels in class tonight. This is great, because the advanced yogins can help the beginners, and the beginners in the room can help remind the more advanced practitioners about the benefits of slowing down and returning to the basics."

- "There may be poses in class tonight that are outside your physical ability. We have students at different levels, with some who might want the challenge, and some who do not. Please listen to your body, and know that I will always give you a modification if you need one. We have lots of props, so you can still do a version of the pose. It's important to try the modification in order to make progress. So if for any reason I don't see you and you need a modification, please call me over so I can help you!"

- "We've got many different levels in class tonight, so you'll see me giving different options for a few poses. Please pay attention to which option is right for you. Some of us are more flexible in certain poses than in others, and some were born with bodies that do certain things that others do not. It's important not to take any of it personally — just have fun with the option that is right for you, and do it with finesse!"

In your own practice, when you do advanced poses, always keep in mind how you would present them in a mixed-ability class. Think about modifications or alternative variations, and practice them so that you can assist the stiffer students with those variations.

During class, scan the room frequently to assess the ability levels in the class. If you see students struggling, make it a point to smile at them and give them encouragement and stabilizing assists without making them feel as if you're singling them out.

By all means, compliment the more advanced students as well, and give them added tips to help them go even deeper, but do it quietly.

If you demonstrate an advanced pose, acknowledge that some students might feel intimidated after seeing it. Then explain and demonstrate the baby steps they can take to eventually get there.

Empower the students with a sequence of poses that make a similar shape to the final, more advanced asana you are building up to. For example, supta padangustasana with the leg out to the side is a similar shape to triangle pose, only you lie on your back. If the students lie on their backs and perform the first pose successfully, they will feel more prepared when you bring them up to do triangle pose standing on their feet.

Be as excited about presenting easier poses as you are about presenting more advanced ones, so you make it clear that one pose or variation is not better than the other. This way the students will feel good about all the asanas, not just the super-bendy poses!

Timing

Value your students' time. Time is one of the most precious commodities we have. Nothing puts students off more than their time being wasted. They gave up a million other things to be in class with you. Be punctual! Start and end class on time. In addition, pay attention to these areas:

- *Opening talk:* Make it short and to the point. State your theme, and then get your students moving within three to five minutes of starting class.
- *Warm-up:* This should be just long enough to get people prepared for the more challenging poses to come.
- *Inversions:* If you bring a group to the wall and need to work with beginners on fundamentals, the more experienced students may finish quickly and get bored. Give them additional poses or variations to work on so that you can give more time to your beginners.
- *Demos:* An effective demo can be a great use of time, saving you a lot of time explaining things, but keep it brief and clear.
- *Holding poses:* Your students are bound to have varying levels of stamina for holding poses. Whether it's a plank or utkatasana (fierce pose), let students know what benefits they might be getting from the hold so that they stay motivated, and of course give them an alternative if they cannot go the distance.
- *Cool-down:* This needs to be like Goldilocks's bed — not too long, not too short, but just right.
- *Savasana:* As a general rule, allow six to seven minutes for savasana — a minute for getting into the pose, five minutes in it, and a minute to come out. If you are teaching a forty-five- or sixty-minute class, you can make it shorter, but always allow at least three minutes for students to lie still in final relaxation.

CHAPTER TWELVE

Teaching Online Skillfully

When you're embarking on teaching online yoga, it's important to know how it differs from teaching in person. One significant difference is that it's nearly impossible for you to "read the room," as there is little or no way to read signals or get real-time feedback from your students online.

All of the following in-person assessments are missing altogether or greatly diminished from the online experience:

- Ability to observe facial expressions
- Ability to hear the quality of the students' breath, groaning, or spontaneous questions because the students are on mute
- Ability to see whether the students are sweating
- Ability to walk around a student 360 degrees, or at least see them from multiple angles, to observe their form

Think about when you teach in person. What are some sounds you hear that indicate you're pushing the students to their limit and it might be time for a child's pose? Perhaps it's panting, groaning, or heavy breathing.

What are some of the visual signs that indicate the pose you chose was too challenging for the majority and that it might be time to offer modifications? Perhaps it's a strained face, some side-eye, or even eye-rolling.

What is a visible sign that your vinyasa flow is intensely vigorous and it might be time to give the students a pause? Perhaps it's heavy perspiration or sweat forming a puddle on the student's mat.

All these signs and cues are missing when you're in a livestream and completely absent with on-demand videos.

Conversation and in-person interaction can tell you a lot about what the students might need to work on in practice, what life challenges they are going through, and what injuries they have. With online yoga there is much less (or no) opportunity for socializing or relationship building, which typically occurs in person before and after class in the studio or lounge. Without this information gathering, it can be harder to tailor a class theme or choose a focus that will serve the students who come to class.

The Importance of Preparation

As you can see, without being able to read the room, spontaneity is not as much of an option — especially with on-demand content. As such, the need to prepare and plan your classes ahead of time is imperative for online instruction.

Planning is so vital because when a student attends a class online it can be much harder to hold their attention. When they are in a room full of other students, they are more accountable to being present and working through any resistance to stick with it to the end, whereas at home, distractions abound. No one is holding them to account, so whenever they want, they can turn off their cameras and leave the meeting or stop the video and attend to a child, put a load of laundry in the dryer, or decide they'd prefer to go outside for a walk!

Teachers who "freestyle" or riff when teaching their on-demand classes tend to get fewer clicks and poor completion rates compared with those whose classes show they are prepared.

To mitigate student drop-off, teach engaging classes that hold attention. The best way to do that is through thorough preparation, deliberate teaching, and meticulous class planning. This means:

- being even more concise in your instruction, story-telling, and introductory dharma talks. Make sure you rehearse delivering your dharma talk or story with minimal words.

- having a written sequence of poses to keep the class moving, and being aware of what poses in the list are least essential and could be scratched if you run out of time.

- having a list of the props needed for class, which you share with the students in advance of the practice or announce at the beginning of class, and having those props ready by your mat.

- looking at your sequence and being cognizant of modifications you're ready to share if the pose is not accessible to certain students. Is there an easier variation they can do? Are there props they can use to aid them in the pose?

- working out ahead of time how you will introduce the class. Particularly for shorter-format on-demand videos, you may even want to script the introductions consistently. For example, "Welcome. Thank you for showing up to practice with me! This class is designed to _____. Let's get started in cat-cow."

- considering what "self-assists" you can teach the students, such as turning their thighs inward in a seated pose.

- rehearsing your classes ahead of time to make sure your sequence and theme make sense.

- having a plan in place for the students so they know how to get your attention if they need help with modifications or have questions. At the beginning of class, I like to state that students have permission to unmute themselves whenever they need to. This not only helps students get their questions answered, but also lets them alert you to tech problems, such as faulty audio, slide presentations not advancing on your screen share, and more! It's especially helpful if you're on your mat and can't see the chat on your computer (and you're without a helper in the meeting room who could otherwise manage that for you).

The good news about all this planning? If you share what you're planning in advance (whether at the end of the current class, in an email, or on social media), your students will be sure to mark their calendars and commit to attending if they are excited about the upcoming topics!

IMPROVISING YOGA PROPS

One of the joys of the Covid pandemic was seeing into everyone's homes through the screen in online meetings, being introduced to people's pets and kids, and most of all, figuring out how they could scrounge up props from household items visible in the background.

For students who don't have their own set of yoga props:

- Couch cushions or rolled-up blankets can be used in place of bolsters.
- When there's not a wall accessible in the practice space, legs-up-the-wall pose can be done with the legs up on a sofa or the back of a chair.
- Books make a great substitute for yoga blocks.
- A belt, scarf, or resistance band can be used instead of a yoga strap.

Demonstration Teaching and Observation Teaching in Livestream Classes

There are two different ways to teach a livestream yoga class. I call one method "demonstration teaching" and the other "observation teaching."

Demonstration Teaching

Demonstration teaching is when the teacher leads the class almost entirely from the yoga mat and practices the poses while giving instruction.

Demonstration teaching is the more typical and widely

used method of the two. Many teachers who were the kind to walk around the room while instructing in-person classes shifted to demonstration teaching when it came to livestream classes because of the students' need for a "visual" when practicing alone at home. And it makes a lot of sense for vinyasa flow yoga, which is more widely practiced and doesn't require as much attention to alignment and form as other styles of yoga.

There are benefits and certain things to keep in mind with this method.

BENEFITS

- The teacher is visible in the poses the entire time, making it easier for the students to model themselves after the teacher.
- The teacher can articulate the instructions from a more embodied place, since they're also doing the poses. This can make it easier to give instructions clearly.
- The teacher can be a little creative, since they're experiencing the practice in the moment and therefore can "throw in" what might feel good to them personally.
- Students who want to take advantage of the anonymity online yoga affords can turn off their camera, since the teacher isn't watching them anyway.
- Although demonstration teaching is no substitute for the teacher doing their own yoga practice (because they're still teaching and concentrating), there's no doubt that it allows teachers to move, stretch, and maintain a certain level of yoga fitness as they teach.

Keep in Mind

- Because the teacher is on their mat, away from the screen, they can't observe the students and check on how they are doing. Being unsupervised can put students at greater risk of injury.

- There is less accountability among the students to be present with the teachings, to put extra effort into their practice, or to be curious about how they might enhance their practice, since no one is looking. Some may even walk away from the mat altogether and leave class early rather than sticking with it.

- Students don't grow in their practice as quickly, and they can get accustomed to unproductive or incorrect patterns of alignment, because no one is giving them individualized feedback on how they could go deeper, be safer, or work with an injury.

- When demonstrating and doing the poses while teaching, the teacher can more easily give real-time instructions, but this can be a missed opportunity to hone the rare skill of delivering concise, easy-to-follow teachings, and as a result, students may need to crane their necks to look at the screen to know what's going on.

Observation Teaching

Observation teaching is when the teacher stands or sits close to the screen with their eyes on the students' videos, giving instruction as well as feedback based on what they are observing. They can use "gallery view" to see all the students arranged as squares in a grid, and they can enlarge the image of a particular student to be able to see that student in detail. When they want to give students a visual of the pose or prop setup they're instructing, teachers can "spotlight" a student in the class, and that student will appear on the screen for the entire class to see. Typically teachers will only spotlight students who they know well, who they know can competently demonstrate the pose, and/or who have given the teacher permission to be spotlighted. When no one is spotlighted, the students see their teacher on the screen as a "talking head."

However, the teacher is not limited to being a talking head for the entire class if a demonstration is needed, and some may choose a hybrid of demonstration teaching and observation teaching. In this case, they would practice alongside the students on their mat and pause periodically to sit close to the screen and observe the students doing what they just taught.

Observation teaching is most appropriate for alignment-based yoga classes, teacher training, and private lessons. As with demonstration teaching, there are pros and cons.

BENEFITS

- As in in-person classes, the teacher can look at each student to make sure the students are safe, following instructions, and practicing to their full potential.
- The teacher can give valuable individual and group feedback based on what they see.
- Students tend to grow and evolve in their practice more quickly, since they are getting regular feedback.
- The teacher can help potentially prevent injury because they can see if the students are at risk of hurting themselves.

- Students are more accountable, put more effort into their practice, and stay present from beginning to end of class, since they know they are being seen.
- The teacher naturally hones the skill of giving precise, easy-to-follow instructions. They often get so good that the students can totally relax, knowing they'll be guided without having to strain to see the screen. In fact, when observation livestream teaching is done well, experienced students can follow along with the audio instruction only and don't need to look at the screen often.

KEEP IN MIND

- If the teacher is not well versed in giving clear, precise instructions (when not also on the mat doing yoga), the students could get very confused, since they don't have a visual of the teacher.
- Certain students may not gravitate toward a teacher who observation teaches because they are used to the more common demonstration teaching and prefer anonymity.
- Because the teacher is not doing the poses along with the students, they miss out on the opportunity to move and stretch and need to schedule that for another time.

Engagement, Retention, and Best Practices When Teaching Digitally

Perhaps one of the most critical aspects of teaching yoga online is keeping your students engaged and coming back for more via the online medium. Understanding this and teaching online classes accordingly is crucial to making your classes stand out.

When I first started teaching on-demand classes in 2012, I tended to be as talkative and wordy as I was when teaching in person. Fortunately, technology and data do not lie. The classes where I talked less performed better, meaning people not only took the class more, but — here's the clincher — they also *finished* the video and didn't hit the stop button. Keep in mind that the retention rate for students is vastly higher if they complete your videos. Incompletion of a video equates, more times than not, to a dissatisfied student!

When people attend classes in person, they are sitting in a room full of other students, and there's a community feeling as the teacher introduces the topic, tells a story, or reads from a text. They have carved out the time to get to and from the studio as well as the time to take the class. The people in the room lift each other up and help hold the collective attention.

With digital yoga, the person practicing is not at the studio because they are trying to save time commuting there and back, plus making themselves presentable (washing their face, brushing their teeth, doing their hair, etc.). They are usually alone on their mat at home in a bedroom or living room.

When a class is not engaging for any reason and doesn't hold their interest, the student can simply turn off their camera, stop the video, or leave the online meeting relatively unnoticed. To put it plainly, their attention span is much shorter than when they're in person.

By contrast, it would take a lot of dissatisfaction for someone to roll up their mat and walk out of a room full of people in the middle of an in-person class, after everything it took to get there. But without the accountability, the only thing keeping the digital student there is *you* and the quality of your teaching!

After working in the online yoga space for over a decade, I can share some best practices to help keep your classes engaging and your retention high — for both livestream and on-demand classes.

Livestream Classes

Teach with an animated, melodic voice, not a monotone. There is nothing quite as unengaging in a movement class as a monotonous teacher. It's neither motivating, captivating, nor persuasive. Instead, a teacher with a more melodic voice can pump up the students during intense moments like holding a challenging pose for another two breaths. They can tone down their voice when there's a moment of pause. The vocal variety is what captivates the students in your class. That said, don't confuse this more engaging, melodic voice with "yoga voice," a sugary, "ultra-spiritual," affected voice that is not authentic to the teacher.

Get the movement practice started sooner and limit long intros or dharma talks. Without being buoyed by an in-person group, online students likely have little to zero patience for long and wordy introductions. They want to move, get their yoga in for the day, and get back to the demands of their home or work life. Therefore, provide a short, well-thought-out welcome to the students, express gratitude, share what they can expect in the practice, and/or briefly introduce the theme. For a sixty-minute class, keep this introduction no longer than three minutes. Remember, you can always elaborate more on the theme once they are in motion.

Talk less. Because of the decreased attention span of online yoga students, too much talking can make the students tune out, whereas if you give them more space and moments of silence, they can get into a zone and into their bodies. Remember, since you're not able to read the room, it can be tough to know if what you're saying is landing with the students, so err on the side of being quieter, and allow the students' experience of themselves to be the main attraction. Aim for fewer, but more impactful, words and instruction.

Be yourself! When you're the only one talking and everyone else is on mute, it can feel like you're teaching into a black hole. The first few times I taught like this were extremely awkward, and I found it hard to be my usual goofball self. I had to laugh at my own jokes and find a way to let my personality come through. Eventually, when I looked at the screen, I could see a handful of students giving me visual signs like thumbs up, hands clapping, or doubling over laughing (God bless the kind students who could tell I was struggling), and I realized they were still feeling me through the digital void! It affirmed for me that just because that void is there doesn't mean I can't break through it and be myself. When in doubt, amuse yourself, and you'll probably amuse everyone else.

If you still feel awkward no matter what you do, try recruiting a friend or family member to be in the room taking class with you if you can, and teach them along with everyone tuning in from home!

If you have a sense of humor, now is the time to use it! As with the above point, this goes without saying. Just because the digital void is there doesn't mean you can't be your usual witty self. Just because it's a yoga class doesn't mean it has to be serious. There's nothing wrong with keeping people smiling, laughing, and entertained while they're practicing.

Build community. The good news with livestream is that you do still have real people showing up for class in the meeting room! Here you can get conversations going before and after class. In workshop or training programs, you can use the breakout room feature to group smaller numbers of people into their own rooms to check in, converse, or practice drills together. We saw students make lifelong friendships in those breakout rooms, friends who later traveled to meet each other in real life afterward!

Greet your students by name. As people arrive to the meeting for class, when you see them in the participants list or on video, give them a personal welcome such as, "Oh yay, Alan is here! So good to see you!" or, "Hey Marissa, welcome!" It can be isolating at home, so when the teacher mentions the student by name, it gives the student a feeling of belonging.

Smile, stay engaged, and be interested. There's something about being in an online meeting that makes people's faces look disinterested. We've all been in a meeting when someone's got a "resting grump" face. If they were in person, they'd somehow be better about looking attentive and interested! As a presenter (particularly in lecture scenarios where your face is close to the camera), be sure to fight this tendency and put a gentle smile on your face. When it's not your turn to talk, stay present and nod your head to indicate you're listening.

Avoid looking off camera or multitasking on your device, as tempting as it is to have all those apps you could be looking at so close by.

Graciously handle cameo appearances from family and pets. During the pandemic a certain amount of "professionalism" went out the window when we were suddenly forced to conduct business out of our homes. Although it's forgivable, and even endearing, when a cat's tail swooshes by someone's downward dog, or a toddler's face comes right up to the camera in the middle of savasana, it's important not to let cameos become too much of a distraction. Do your best to take preventative action to avoid familial or pet disruptions on your end, but if one happens anyway, don't make it a huge deal — just smile, laugh, and carry on. Your students will understand.

Teach from the heart and keep classes relevant to the times. Digital yoga can at times feel sterile and devoid of real human interaction. One way to lessen that is to present from your heart and bring in themes that reflect what's going on in the world (more on this in chapter 14) to build human connection. If it helps, sit for meditation before class and tune in to your emotional body so you can drop into what's most meaningful to you in the moment and share your heart with the students.

Teach self-assists. Since it's not possible to give hands-on assists in a livestream class, do the next best thing! Teach the students to use their hands to give themselves assists. Here are a few that come to mind:

- In pigeon pose, pressing down on the root of the femur of the bent leg to anchor it.
- In various seated poses, giving each thigh an internal rotation.
- When trying for a bind in revolved extended side angle, using your top hand to rotate the forearm in and upper arm out before clasping both hands together.
- In ankle-to-knee pose, giving each thigh an internal rotation and then anchoring the tops of the femurs with your hands before hinging forward.

Teach strategically from a marketing/community perspective.
Just as with in-person classes, teaching from a marketing perspective means that you share your upcoming offerings with your students during class, not just as an announcement at the beginning or end. For example, if you have a lower-back workshop coming up, focus part of your class on freeing up the lower back in seated poses and twists. In the moment, let the students know you'll be going into greater depth on this topic in your upcoming livestream workshop. To encourage community gathering (and peer pressure!), ask people to raise their hand if they already signed up. Tell them you'll pop the link to register into the chat before they go.

Similarly, don't hesitate to refer to teachings you gave in the previous class, such as, "Remember last week, when we worked on getting our groins back in press handstands? Let's use that same idea here." Anyone who missed it is bound to feel a little FOMO (fear of missing out) and may vow to attend class more consistently moving forward.

When you do make announcements at the end of class,

let people in on what you have planned for the next class and why it will benefit them. They'll be sure to put it in their calendar!

Use the chat for students to convey feedback on how poses felt. In my quest to know what the students are experiencing in my livestream classes, I will take a moment after a more challenging pose to ask attendees to come over to their devices and type into the chat or unmute themselves to tell me how they experienced the pose or action. The students seem to enjoy having a voice and interaction rather than feeling like they're practicing in a vacuum!

Build trust by being on time. Everyone is busy and distracted these days. It's a blessing to be able to reach students across space and time with a livestream class. To respect everyone's time and build trust, it's imperative you start and end the classes on time.

Demonstrate accordingly for basic-level classes. When teaching basic-level classes, be aware of how a student at that level might practice. Would their knees be bent in downward dog and standing forward fold? Would their knees be up high sitting cross-legged or in baddha konasana? Put yourself in their shoes and be sure to model accordingly and approachably for the folks who have shown up live and the newbies who might watch the recording later.

Do your best to mimic what it's like to be in an in-person yoga class. There's nothing like practicing yoga in person, but we can certainly make the most out of what virtual yoga has to offer. If you follow the tips above and build community, you will succeed in bringing much of the best of in-person yoga to the screen.

Prerecorded/On-Demand Content

Most of the best practices for creating engagement in livestream classes are also applicable to filming on-demand content, but there is some nuance.

Build connection. Although there are on-demand classes with "studio students" who can be with you on the mat, most on-demand content is filmed with just the teacher and their mat. Without anyone practicing alongside you live, it can be easy to go into your own world and forget that you will have an audience of practitioners. Compared to livestream teaching, on-demand teaching has an even bigger "void" — there is literally no one there to react to your teaching.

Students who take on-demand classes are the most isolated because they're doing so on their own time, by themselves. To build a sense of connection, be as genuine as possible. That is, be the same person on camera as off camera, and students will gravitate to you and your content. If you have a sense of humor, use it.

Smile often and speak to the camera directly as you give instructions. I often imagine that the students are all inside the camera lens! Sometimes in an asana, you must turn your head to look at the camera when you normally would not. Though this may feel awkward or forced, your smile, positive encouragement, and direct eye contact will draw the students in. For example, you might be in a crescent lunge with the camera showing your profile. Normally your gaze (*drishti*) would be straight ahead, but to create better engagement with the audience, shift your gaze to the camera as you're giving instructions on how to hold the pose, and smile. Depending on your comfort level, saying things like, "Keep breathing, you're doing great," or, "Hang in there, you got this!" during more challenging asanas can go a long way in motivating a student to stick with the practice.

Consider filming shorter-duration classes, especially fifteen-minute to thirty-minute classes. The luxury of the on-demand modality is that you can offer shorter-format, micro practices, perfect for the non–yoga studio crowd who would rather get in fifteen minutes of yoga than none at all. And in fact, it is always healthier to get in some activity than to be sedentary. Also, one of the big reasons that students do online yoga is they simply don't have time, and therefore building short practices to fit into their busy schedule is essential.

Keep dharma talks and intros to a minimum. I know I sound like a broken record, but keep in mind that the attention spans of students taking on-demand classes is even shorter than those of livestream students. When you film shorter-format practices (between five and thirty minutes), you'll want to shorten your introductions even more.

I suggest keeping your intro brief and to the point, aiming for thirty seconds or less. You could say something as streamlined as, "Welcome. This practice will wind down your day and prepare you for sleep. Let's get started."

When you close the practice, clearly indicate the ending so it's not awkward. You can simply say, "Thank you for practicing," with your hands in prayer and bow your head.

Demonstration teach, since you can't give feedback anyway! This is stating the obvious, but in on-demand classes, there's no one for you to observe, so you might as well provide a constant visual and the feeling that you're practicing together with your audience. Therefore, stay on your mat the whole time.

Teach with an animated, melodic voice rather than a monotone. As with livestream teaching, be aware of your delivery, and when you fall into a monotone, change up your voice!

Keep people moving. Avoid stopping the flow to break down poses. Keep the class moving and in constant action. To be clear, a quiet pause in a child's pose would be considered "in action," whereas stopping and talking about a pose would not. The only times you might stop a flow to talk about a pose are (a) if you are filming a tutorial (such as, "Build a Better Downward Dog" or "What to Do with Your Neck in Camel Pose") or (b) the class is building to a peak pose, and the peak pose needs a little bit of explaining when you get to it.

Talk less. Easy-to-follow instructions with some quiet space in between work best for on demand. This means being economical with your language to avoid overexplaining poses or stalling the class to break poses down. You want to be as precise with your placement instructions as possible (see page 178) so that students don't need to look at the screen to know what to do. This is true when teaching in-person classes too, but it's especially crucial for on-demand content.

Model appropriately for the level of the class. As with live-stream classes, in basic-level videos, be a relatable model. To foster belonging and inclusion, you should aim to model poses to the level of the class. You may opt to showcase a more intense range of motion and demonstration options to more advanced-level classes.

Build trust by staying within the specified time. In this case, starting and ending on time is not relevant, since the students will be taking the class on their own schedule. However, you will want to keep your videos true to a consistent time block like five, ten, fifteen, twenty, or thirty minutes. This means a ten-minute practice is truly ten minutes, and a thirty-minute practice is truly thirty minutes. Typically, you'll want to stay within thirty seconds of the allotted time for short practices (five, ten, or fifteen minutes) and within sixty seconds for longer-format practices.

It's also best to avoid referring to time during class. For example, avoid saying, "We'll stay in this restorative pose for ten minutes." Students who practice on-demand classes could hold you to that exact time, and you might not be able to be that precise. Instead, you can give them an approximate time, such as, "We'll stay in this restorative pose for the next few minutes."

Hybrid Classes

Hybrid classes are now a normal part of yoga studio culture. Many studios are still set up with their livestream production equipment from the pandemic and are catering to students who prefer to beam in from home. You may be asked to teach a hybrid class, in which case, keep these guidelines in mind:

- If you are responsible for handling technology and production equipment, give yourself plenty of time to get the studio set up before class, and work with production checklists so all the details are taken care of.

- Technology and equipment can be frustrating and can fail when we need them most. Be patient and calm when things go wrong.
- Do your best to give attention to everyone — both the folks beaming in and the students in the room.
- Keep in mind that a larger monitor will make it easier for you to see the students at home and therefore more natural for you to include them in your instructions and feedback. If you're working with a smaller monitor, you will want to make an extra effort not to forget about the folks at home.

A WORD ON SAVASANA ON DEMAND

There's a joke going around that a unicorn dies whenever someone skips savasana. And, well, savasana is vital in fostering the rejuvenation and integration we need to support our practice and our nervous systems. However, with micro-format classes online that have a target outcome and students who tend to be pressed for time, you might need to skip savasana in favor of giving students a practice with a full range of poses. However, all is not lost, as you can give students the option to rest in savasana if they have the time.

You could say something like, "If you're able, take as long as you like in savasana now, and for those who need to go, we'll close here." If you do opt to include a brief savasana, end the class on time but give the students the option to stay in savasana as long as they like before guiding everyone else out of savasana and closing the class.

ChatGPT/AI and Your Yoga Business

Artificial intelligence (AI) is all around us, whether we notice it or not. Every time an unwanted email is blocked by your spam filter, every time you watch a movie Netflix recommended for you, every time your bank flags suspicious activity on your account, you are reaping the benefits of AI.

In early 2023, a new kind of artificial intelligence called generative AI captured the public attention thanks to a product called ChatGPT. Combining natural language processing with a massive set of training data, generative AI can independently create original new content, including images, audio, and text, based on the data it is trained to interpret. ChatGPT shocked even its creators with its ability to interact in a conversational style, to seemingly understand human language, and to perform tasks previously impossible to do with AI.

In the months after the release of ChatGPT, additional similar programs were rolled out (such as Microsoft Bing's AI and Google Bard). Though we focus here on ChatGPT because it's the most well known at this point, the following information applies to similar generative AI platforms as well.

What does this mean for yoga teachers and studio owners? If used correctly, ChatGPT can open new opportunities to engage your audience and reduce time spent on day-to-day administrative tasks.

What You Can Use It For

ChatGPT has an uncanny capacity to grasp the nuances of language, context, and intent, making it a powerful tool for interactive communication.

For yoga teachers and studios, ChatGPT can be your

virtual writing assistant, creating blog posts, newsletters, articles, social media captions, and video scripts and shot lists. It can be your collaborator if you use it to brainstorm ideas, draft content, and even proofread, improve, and edit your written material. It can summarize long documents or articles you don't have time to read, provide an Instagram posting strategy, or give you yoga retreat marketing ideas. Even smaller uses, like asking it to suggest a few other ways of saying something or asking for music suggestions to use as a background for your Instagram Reel, can be a game changer in terms of time savings.

You can also ask ChatGPT for help suggesting tailored yoga practices/sequences with consideration for factors such as student skill level, health, injuries, and countless yoga class outcomes such as stress relief, morning yoga, specific areas of the body, and more.

As a small business owner, you may wish you had a personal help desk. Well, now you do: Describe what you want an Excel formula to do, and ChatGPT can write it for you. Not sure how to blur your Zoom background? Just ask ChatGPT.

It can also plan travel itineraries, suggest locations for retreats, and even translate your work into other languages.

What Not to Use It For

As with any new technology, but particularly one that can write for you or help plan your yoga class, you must proceed with caution. Generative AI is prone to something called "hallucinations" — in other words, making things up. It is particularly prone to hallucinating in response to math questions and with information about individual people. It is therefore critical that you never assume that what it spits out is factually correct. If you are not sure, verify with an independent source. And although other GenAI tools like Google Bard and Microsoft Bing's AI have access to current information, ChatGPT is only trained up to September 2021 and has no information about the world after that date, so it can't advise you on current events.

Prompt Engineering

Prompt engineering is the art of adjusting your ChatGPT prompts (questions or inputs) in such a way that they help the AI model understand your request and provide a more relevant response. Taking the time to learn some prompting basics can radically improve the results you get. A few tips to get you started:

- Make your prompts specific:

  o Request an exact length. Ask for "a 3-sentence summary" not "a short summary."

  o Tell it to "write a 2-paragraph summary or caption," or a "100-word summary or caption."

  o Tell it to write at an eighth-grade reading level, which will generate text that is accessible to general audiences.

- Ask for rewrites if you don't like the output:

  o Tell it what kind of person the expected reader is.

  o Tell it to use a certain tone (more enthusiastic, more hip, less casual).

  o For content that is too long, tell it to "write it again but 20% shorter."

  o If you want to avoid any particular terminology,

tell it to "rewrite the response but this time, don't use the phrase _____."

Using ChatGPT Responsibly

Having a business concierge like ChatGPT might seem like a dream come true, offering significant time savings and convenience. However, it also raises crucial concerns regarding the absence of human interaction and the potential impact on our cognitive capabilities. While the allure of efficiency is enticing, we must carefully consider the trade-offs and ensure that we strike a balance between the benefits of AI and the value of human presence and critical thinking. Here are some areas to consider in an effort to strike the appropriate balance:

- *Accuracy and personalization:* While ChatGPT is smart, it can't possibly grasp every student's individual needs, state of health, and body type. Relying solely on AI may lead to inappropriate guidance. It can't understand the context or nuances of yoga poses and instructions accurately. Balancing AI assistance and personalized teaching is vital for safe and effective teaching.
- *Authenticity:* Yoga teachers have their own style of teaching, writing, and intuition that makes their classes and content distinct. Overreliance on ChatGPT could make your content sound unoriginal. I've used ChatGPT to assist me in writing marketing copy enough that I can usually tell when a yoga organization has used it without tweaking it to be more genuine, because I recognize some of the cliché words it

often spits out, such as "transformational," "journey," and "unleash!"

- *Avoiding overdependency:* It's essential not to become overly reliant on ChatGPT and to keep your own critical thinking and creativity intact. Use ChatGPT to help get you started or to provide a framework for your writing, but then edit, edit, edit to make it your own.

- *Yoga philosophy and ethics:* Some might question whether integrating AI aligns well with the traditional yoga philosophy of self-awareness and *satya* (truthfulness), particularly in the context of yoga teacher trainings (for more about this, see the box below). If this question resonates with you, you might consider discussing it in a dharma talk or spurring a discussion about it on social media.

AI AND YOGA TEACHER TRAININGS

If you are a teacher trainer giving written assignments to your trainees, they could very easily have ChatGPT write their papers, which could hinder them from developing their research, critical thinking, and writing skills. Writing allows trainees to express the thoughts, reflections, and insights they gain during their training. Depending on AI for their written assignments could stifle their personal growth as yoga teachers as well as rob them of a deeper connection to or understanding of the teachings. When I was in teacher training, engaging in discussions, seeking guidance from my teacher, and collaborating with my peers was a big part of what inspired me and my writing. AI could discourage trainees from that more interactive learning environment.

To address these concerns, clearly communicate the expectations for paper writing and emphasize the importance of independent research and critical thinking. It might help to foster open discussions about AI, its applications, and its limitations, promoting ethical use and responsible AI practices. Talk about how to use it as a tool for learning. Explain the value of doing your own thinking and writing; I like using the analogy that "riding an e-bike around the Tour de France route won't give you the fitness you need to compete in it."

Have a policy for when and where the use of GenAI is appropriate. For example, you might even encourage students to use ChatGPT to stimulate creative thinking and brainstorming but not to write assignments outright. You might have them use it to grasp the basics of a complex idea or a challenging concept, then build on it once they feel comfortable. Or you might allow students for whom English is a second language to use ChatGPT for a spelling and grammar check of content written in English.

As most yoga teacher trainings do, be sure to incorporate plenty of opportunities for interactive learning, group discussions, and peer collaborations to maintain an engaging and supportive learning environment.

What to Do When Students Cheat

If you suspect that students are using ChatGPT as a substitute for independent thought, talk to them. Ask how they came up with their ideas. Ask them to elaborate on concepts in their content.

If it's more widespread than one or two people, consider using class time for active discussion instead of written assignments so that you can observe the students' thought processes in real time. You could even require proctored exams completed in person or over Zoom.

In summary, ChatGPT can be a valuable resource for yoga professionals, but it's vital to use it mindfully. Being aware of the concerns and striking a healthy balance will help you make the most of generative AI while staying true to the heart of yoga.

Part IV

LEADING BY EXAMPLE

CHAPTER THIRTEEN

Self-Care

In chapter 10, we talked about the teaching "container," or *dharana*. Throughout this book, we've been discussing all the things that should be in your teaching container: your values and mission statement, good time-management and scheduling, healthy personal and professional relationships, and ways to secure your finances and your ability to contribute as you'd like.

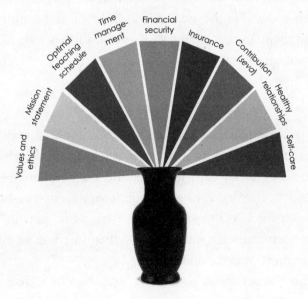

These things don't just magically appear in your container: you have to put them there.

We have now looked at every segment shown above except *self-care*. To put it simply, teaching well requires that you are well, and you can truly be well only when you take good care of yourself through healthy habits.

Please don't assume that we are talking about self-care toward the end of the book because it isn't that important. It is.

The sign of a great teacher is one who "walks the talk." It's not enough to preach wellness and healthy habits; you want to live them to such an extent that you are a role model for others. (This doesn't mean you should become so pure in your eating and health habits that no one can relate to you. We are not talking about extremes.)

Imagine taking a class with a teacher who is vibrantly alive, who glows, who obviously attends to their mental, emotional, and physical health. This shows in how they talk, how they listen, how they look and feel. A person in this state has a twinkle in their eye and is irresistibly appealing; you just want to be around them. In this section we'll look at various ways to nurture yourself so that you can give your best to your students.

Your Own Yoga Practice

Have you ever taken a yoga class when you could just tell that the teacher was not into it? Or have you been that teacher? A passionless teacher can't inspire students. Fortunately, there is a remedy, and that is to get on your own yoga mat and meditation cushion. As the yogini Dana Trixie Flynn puts it, "Just as a concert musician must practice their instrument, a yoga teacher must practice on their mat."

This doesn't mean going to a workshop or retreat only

once in a while — though that can be nice — and coming back inspired and enthusiastic. This is about continual refueling. It means getting on your yoga mat consistently, at home, in a class, or at a practice for teachers and advanced students.

This may seem obvious, but the majority of teachers we've polled complain that their single biggest challenge as a teacher is keeping up their own practice. If this is a problem for you, here are some ideas to get you rolling. If you're practicing consistently already, you can skim this section, but you might consider helping to uplift the whole teaching community by organizing group practices that help others stay motivated too.

Establish — and Maintain — Your Home Practice

Having a practice of your own can be not only empowering but often incredibly creative and innovative. If you don't continue to practice regularly in addition to teaching, your only source of inspiration for your teaching is the stale memory of a regular practice. Do whatever it takes to get yourself on your mat five to seven days a week, even if only for a short time. Put on your favorite music first thing in the morning, and get on your mat and just experiment with movement.

Vow to practice at least ten minutes a day, five to seven days a week. By committing to only ten minutes, you avoid putting pressure on yourself, and you're more likely to stick to the resolution. If you start small, you will find yourself craving more time on the mat.

Create a dedicated space in your home for your practice (perhaps, like many yogins, you did this during the pandemic). This will encourage you to practice at home more often. It doesn't have to be anything special — and you certainly don't want to put so much thought into it that the planning process prevents you from rolling out your mat! But when you put just enough energy into a space, it can become magnetic, drawing you onto the mat.

Other tips for practicing consistently and keeping your practice interesting include the following:

- Go straight from your bed to the mat in the morning
- Queue up new music to listen to while practicing
- Attempt a new pose and do a warm-up that gets you there
- Practice someplace new — in a different room, outside, or even in a hot tub
- Lay out your mat in an unavoidable space
- Set a goal for the week, such as a certain number of days on the mat, a certain pose, or more time in a pose
- Keep an asana and meditation journal to stay accountable to yourself
- Write down any inspiring sequences you've done in other teachers' classes or practices, and work on them again

Regularly Practice with Other Teachers

Practicing yoga with other teachers is a vital, synergistic way to build up your yoga practice.

In 2001, I started teaching classes at Laughing Lotus Yoga Center in New York City, founded by the New York yoginis Dana Trixie Flynn and Jasmine Tarkeshi. What I loved about Dana's class was that even after years of teaching yoga, she never seemed to run out of enthusiasm or creativity in her presentations. The excitement was compelling; it made her classes into events you did not want to miss.

When I wondered about the secret to creating this energy, I learned that Dana was on her mat every day, dancing, experimenting, and creating magic.

Dana and I started practicing together weekly at Laughing Lotus, inviting other teachers to join us. I remember those days fondly. The practice was a laboratory for yoga craziness: learning about our bodies and where we needed to develop strength, where we needed to open up, experimenting with zany poses, making up new ones, figuring out how best to get into advanced poses, and more. We did timings and repetitions, played ridiculous music, and laughed.

That spirit of creativity and togetherness led to some of the biggest breakthroughs in my yoga practice. When I moved to Colorado in 2004 and discovered a teachers' practice called "The Tigress," I felt at home again.

If there's nothing similar in your area, consider organizing your own informal practice for teachers and advanced practitioners. It's a terrific way to advance your practice and keep yoga exciting.

Here are some tips for organizing a teachers' practice:

- Pick a time based on the availability of the teachers in your area, either by doing a survey or doing some online research on teachers' schedules.
- Find a yoga studio to host the practice during off hours, preferably as a community service to the local teachers.
- When you have settled on a location and meeting time, send an email invitation to all the teachers.
- Start a group or create an event page for the practice on social media. Post pictures and even videos to get people inspired. Be consistent and show up yourself. Repeat: *Be consistent and show up yourself!*

- Send out a reminder email the day before each practice, and let the group know what cool things might
  be occurring at the practice, such as holiday or birthday celebrations, or a specific pose the practice will
  build to.
- Celebrate birthdays, holidays, and milestones, and
  regularly dedicate your practices to students in the
  community and anyone in need.
- Choose an experienced teacher to lead the practice
  (it might be you), or have all the teachers take turns
  as leader.

Another way to keep your own practice fresh is to attend
other teachers' classes and workshops in your community.
This not only benefits your yoga practice but also increases
your visibility. Chances are that your attendance at your
peers' classes will be reciprocated. When they come to your
classes, you can mention their presence to your students and
compliment their teaching, showing a spirit of camaraderie,
collaboration, and generosity in the studio.

Mental and Emotional Health

Keeping your mind sharp and clear is key to great teaching.
Unresolved conflicts with people you love or work with can
sap your energy and make you preoccupied and less present
in the classroom.

If you're dealing with unresolved conflicts with family,
friends, colleagues, or others, can you clear the air? How about
your relationship to your significant other? Are you tending
to your partner's needs and expressing your own?

One way to tend to your emotional health and find paths
out of conflict is to keep a journal where you can blow off

steam or vent. Another is to express yourself through art. If you have a creative pastime that you've been neglecting, maybe now is the time to take it up again.

Here are some other options to consider to lift your spirits:

- *Get a massage or bodywork.* After a massage, I feel like I can do anything! Being touched changes my whole mood and outlook on life and makes me want to give back to others.
- *Have a vacation planned.* Knowing that there is a light at the end of the work tunnel can give you a lot more energy.
- *Be more social.* Schedule time to be enriched by the company of friends. If you're in a relationship, plan get-togethers with other friends to enjoy the benefits of community.

Your Physical Appearance and Well-Being

This may seem superficial, but attending to your appearance can make a huge difference to your sense of well-being and self-esteem. A yoga teacher who projects vibrant energy and radiance makes a great role model for health and wellness. Looking and feeling good instantly gives you more professionalism and presence.

Consider these areas:

- *Exercise:* Are you getting ample cardiovascular exercise besides yoga? Moving and getting your heart rate up is invigorating. I recently started learning a new sport, skate skiing. It is very aerobic and works the whole body. It leaves me feeling like an Ironwoman, full of life and uplifted from the sun's reflection on the snow.

- *Diet:* Are you eating clean, nourishing meals?
- *Skin care:* Could your skin glow more? Problem skin may be a sign of a nutritional or sleep deficiency.
- *Hair:* When your hair is nicely styled and cut regularly, you'll come across as more professional.
- *Hygiene:* When you arrive for class looking and feeling fresh, you'll project a more energetic and healthy image. Bring deodorant in your bag in case you have a stinky moment.
- *Feet:* Pedicures are a perfect treat for yoga teachers, since we are barefoot so much of the time, and students do look at our feet.

Taking care of yourself and your appearance can be expensive, but it's an investment in your career and teaching. When you are healthy, vibrant, and looking and feeling good, opportunities come your way, and your classes become more energized.

Organization

As we talk about organizing your teaching, I can't resist adding a note about organizing the rest of your life. Obviously, that's a big subject, but I have seen remarkable results from tackling aspects of it.

Take some time to organize your possessions. If you're sitting in a cluttered office space, it's likely you'll have less energy, lack creativity, and have poor self-esteem. A messy closet can cause you to spend fifteen minutes looking for a misplaced yoga top when you could have been on your mat practicing — or planning a class.

When you declutter your home, you release natural endorphins that give you a surge of pleasure and energy. When my mother inherited my grandmother's possessions, I recommended that she hire a professional organizer to help declutter the house. My mom had done yoga sporadically for years but was not what I'd call a yogini. And yet when she saw what she and the organizer had done in her office, she reported having what I could only call a *kundalini* experience. Decluttering sent a liberating energy through her spine and out the crown of her head, one that gave her a lasting sense of possibility and potential.

I experienced these benefits for myself when my mom gifted me my own session with a professional organizer. I am still using the filing system we set up, I know how and when to purge closets and rooms, and I can keep, toss, and organize much more efficiently. Though I use these systems predominantly in my personal life, they extend into my professional life as well.

CHAPTER FOURTEEN

Leadership and Karma Yoga (Regenerative Practices and Social Change)

One of my most influential teachers always taught me to receive what the world is offering and then decide what to do about it. He taught us not to turn away from the world, but to turn toward it and creatively envision a world we'd like to see.

While a lot is going well in the world today, receiving the rest of what it's offering can feel like drinking from a fire hydrant of worry, despair, fear, and anxiety. It's an understatement to say that there's a lot going on right now. With each passing day it becomes clearer that we are at a watershed moment in history.

Consider just some of the disheartening facts we face and what is at stake:

- Globally, countries are fighting for independence, democracy, and freedom from oppression as authoritarianism, hate, racism, and fascism are on the rise.
- State-sanctioned violence by police continues to be the leading cause of death for young Black men in America.

- Gun violence is the leading cause of death for children and young adults in the United States. In 2021 alone, guns killed more than forty-five thousand Americans, the highest toll in decades.
- Extreme social inequities are increasing, such as the wealth gap, health-care gap, and wellness gap.
- We're facing the magnitude of the climate crisis:
  - Record-breaking temperature highs are causing dangerous heat waves in communities across the globe.
  - Devastating hurricanes and flooding are becoming more common and more intense, displacing millions.
  - Forest fires are decimating wildlife habitat, homes, and businesses all over the world, and with the trees burned, deadly mudslides and floods follow when it rains.
  - People now must deal with not just anxiety but "climate anxiety."
  - The planet's growing uninhabitability will trigger mass human migration, with our most vulnerable populations bearing the brunt of extreme heat and weather events.
- Pandemics from mutating viruses are expected to be the new normal.
- The Amazon rainforest, aka "the lungs of the planet," is being destroyed by wildfire and logging.
- Humans have dumped over 150 million metric tons of plastic in the ocean — you can find the presence of plastic now on even the most remote beaches, and the

    majority of beaches worldwide are covered in plastic
litter.

- Industrial agriculture has poisoned our waters and
depleted our soil of nutrients, so the food we grow
is less nutrient dense and therefore threatens human
health, food security, and food access.
- Human health and essential pollinators face immi-
nent peril due to the relentless, chronic application
of chemical pesticides and herbicides on crops and
home gardens.

I could go on, and on, and on.

Since this book was first published in 2016 many changes
have taken place that have only intensified these issues, and
these changes have impacted the yoga world in turn.

Though social media was a part of our culture when the
book first came out, the algorithms that serve up content into
our feeds according to our individual interests have become
more sophisticated. This has relentlessly polarized people
into silos. Typically, people with differing viewpoints no longer debate or exchange ideas and instead entrench into their
camps, engaging only with those who share similar visions,
viewpoints, and values. We are now harshly divided.

Back in 2016, after I saw one of the workers on our house
project sanding drywall and texting at the same time (insert
facepalm emoji), I told anyone who'd listen how our brains
were getting dumber, our attention spans were vanishing, and
we had better find a way to put our phones down. I even
taught an online course called "Yoga in the Digital Age" to
alert yoga teachers and encourage them to take up the mantle
of helping their students to digitally detox. Fast-forward to
today, and now distraction, brain fog, and inability to focus

are ubiquitous. The difference between 2016 and now is that this societal inability to think critically or understand nuance has created serious long-term consequences in everyday life, from fatal mistakes being made (such as accidents caused by texting while crossing the street), to disinformation leading to loss of life, to burgeoning fascism taking hold in traditionally democratic nations.

In 2020, the Covid-19 pandemic caused wide-scale isolation as lockdowns around the world kept many in quarantine for months on end. I, like many, struggled with depression, lethargy, temporary damage to communication skills (from the lack of human interaction), and grief at the sheer loss of human life in our communities. As we know, the pandemic turned the yoga world upside down, and it is still recovering as it is also reinventing itself.

The year 2020 brought a massive racial reckoning in almost every sector of life and business in America after the murder of George Floyd by a former police officer for suspicion of using a counterfeit twenty-dollar bill. The murder sparked huge protests around the world against systemic racism and police violence. Many also began a journey of inner work to dismantle racism in themselves and to extend that awareness into their families and professions. Folks in the yoga community took a long, hard look at how the wellness world itself had been unknowingly perpetuating and reinforcing racism.

Yoga professionals in far greater numbers than ever began waking up to the truth that the wellness industry has historically been centered on white women, and that whitewashed marketing, devoid of representation and replete with microaggressions, made yoga spaces unwelcoming to Black and Brown practitioners. People realized that luxury pricing common in wellness spaces created sharp and inaccessible barriers to entry. This racial reckoning also shed light on how other underserved communities were also excluded from yoga spaces, including people of size and members of the LGBTQIA+ communities.

The good news is that many yoga professionals and businesses made a commitment to do the real work of looking at their own unconscious biases daily, learning from Black and Brown authors and teachers, and taking action to hire and elevate Black and Brown yoga professionals into positions of leadership. As is to be expected, we also saw many give lip service to the problem with performative posts for the optics, without the real substance, consistent inner work, or commitment to change.

Many yoga professionals came to terms with the definition of wellness they had been reinforcing — that of being superhuman, fit, bendy, or perpetually healthy, youthful, and pain-free (i.e., superior) rather than promoting wellness as a way to find ease within the challenges of life, accessible to all. Gail Parker, PhD, in her book *Restorative Yoga for Ethnic and Race-Based Stress and Trauma,* says that wellness is something "remembered." She writes, "It is the most natural thing in the world. You cannot make it happen, and you don't have to, but you can create conditions that optimize the ability of the body to remember its innate blueprint of order, balance, harmony, and flow."*

Indeed, true wellness is the ability to look inward in order to be of service. Describing great spiritual activists, Parker

---

* Gail Parker, PhD, *Restorative Yoga for Ethnic and Race-Based Stress and Trauma* (London: Jessica Kingsley, 2020), 94.

writes: "What they had in common was consciousness of a power greater than themselves, and they engaged in practices that enabled them to face the storms and problems associated with the work they were called to do.... They practiced change from the inside out by being the change they were advocating for."* This definition is equally applicable to exemplary yoga teachers and something I believe all of us yoga teachers should strive for.

Practicing for self-inquiry and inner quieting is a very different idea of wellness than what we often see online amid videos of privileged, white, and fit people cold-plunging, drinking superfood elixirs, and shooting videos of themselves using skin-care devices. Of course, people are free to partake in these healthy trends, but they do not define wellness.

REVISITING THE PAST AS A WAY TO REPAIR AND REBUILD FOR THE FUTURE

The yoga community reveres the present moment. Yoga teachers prompt their students with affirmations such as "be here now," inviting them to immerse themselves in the present. This perspective makes sense, since being present cultivates well-being by heightening awareness. Some teachers are remarkably passionate about the present moment, viewing dwelling on the past as an attachment, and anticipating the future as a potential trigger for anxiety.

But what if we approached time from a broader perspective? What if we zoomed out enough to see past, present, and future as interdependent and

---

*   Parker, *Restorative Yoga for Ethnic and Race-Based Stress*, 166–67.

interrelated? In Sanskrit, this idea is called *kalapur-nata*, meaning "the fullness of time."

In this model of time, part of living in the present is recognizing that the choices we make now will impact both the near and the far future. And to build a better world, and make better choices, we must also look back to our history and learn from our mistakes.

As the late Sinéad O'Connor wrote in her song "Famine," about the abomination of the Irish famine:

And if there ever is gonna be healing
There has to be remembering
And then grieving
So that there then can be forgiving
There has to be knowledge and understanding

The United States and many places in the world continue to be haunted by atrocity-laden beginnings in conflict with their ideals. I continually remind myself that my country was established and built through the genocide of Indigenous Peoples, stolen land, and enslaved Africans.

Martin Luther King said it most clearly: "Our nation was born in genocide when it embraced the doctrine that the original American, the Indian, was an inferior race. Even before there were large numbers of Negroes on our shore, the scar of racial hatred had already disfigured colonial society. From the sixteenth century forward, blood flowed in battles over racial supremacy. We are perhaps the only nation which tried as a matter of national policy to wipe out its indigenous population."*

---

* Martin Luther King Jr., *Why We Can't Wait* (1963–1964; repr., New York: Signet Classic, 2000), 110.

> When I dwell in the truth of our history, I see it as not something to hide from, "let go of and move on" or "get over already," but as something to feel, and try to repair. Because in order to make a world we want to see, we must address our past and make reparations. We will repeat what we don't acknowledge and rectify.

Yoga's Role in Creating Social and Environmental Change

My teacher always taught that the yoga we were learning was not about checking out; it was about *checking in*. The alternative is what is widely known as *spiritual bypassing*, or using spiritual practice to check out, avoid negative feelings, or escape the reality of what the world is exhibiting.

With so many earth and social woes amassing in the world around us, it can be easy to tune out, go into a state of denial, or become politically apathetic. If you have privilege and means, your safety and basic well-being are much more assured than they are for the majority of folks living in the world, so it's even easier to disengage and become disinterested in current events.

In our scramble to avoid darkness, suffering, politics, ecological collapse, societal upheaval, and oppression in our culture, it can be tempting to make yoga into our happy place, where we don't have to feel any negativity and it's "good vibes only." Many just want to numb themselves. In such tumultuous times, where tragedy just won't stop, people become desensitized.

Given these rough times, many yoga teachers position

their classes as a form of escape or use the practice as a means for tuning out the mess rather than encouraging students to tune in and engage in the madness in a conscious, compassionate way — and most importantly, be creative in finding ways to act to build a better world.

But here's the thing: You can't pray, meditate, or sweat reality away. No amount of yoga retreats, green smoothies, or high-waisted yoga pants will address the world's problems. At best, yoga and meditation practices will let you be more present to darkness or difficulty once you get off your mat. But to declare your practice "free from bad vibes" is a bypass.

When times are tough, I focus my practice even more on "feeling it all" and the desire to send strength and love to those in need. I also recognize that yoga is a powerful practice that can regulate our nervous systems and improve our resiliency, which will prepare us to better handle challenges and enhance all that life has to offer.

In this unprecedented time in our history, ask yourself:

- Do you want your yoga practice to be a way to check out and indulge your need to feel good?
- Is your yoga increasing your sensitivity, emotional awareness, and sensation or aiding you in desensitizing?
- Do you want to absolve yourself of responsibility for what is happening in the world? Or do you want to check in and stay connected to the intricate web of humanity and the world around you?

Staying informed and engaged is not always the easy path, for it involves grief, hurt, and pain, but it is the only path for those willing to grow and be in it for the good of all.

Yoga teacher trainings often teach their trainees to avoid this more difficult path and stay away from bringing current

events or politics into their classes. Which begs the question,
Is addressing politics, negativity, or current events appropriate in the context of teaching yoga?

A WORD ON POLITICS

I'll never forget visiting the remote, pristine islands in
Raja Ampat, Indonesia. We were staying in a beautiful overwater bungalow. However, each day as
the tide came in, it was gut-wrenching to see how
much plastic waste was floating in the water outside
our door. Even there, in what was considered marine wilderness, there was no escape from the plastic
that drifted out from the cities and boats of Indonesia. Each bungalow had a pool skimmer next to it so
guests could help fish the plastic out of the ocean for
proper disposal.

I remember talking with the owner about how
shocking it was to see plastic litter in such a pristine
place. He made the very salient point that it wasn't
enough to try to make people change their behav-
ior on an individual basis (like eliminating single-use
plastic in their day-to-day lives) but that *change in
policy* was the most effective way to create structural
change.

He shared how for a while on the island, multiple
plastic drink cups consistently washed up with the
tides. Once they were able to trace the cups back
to the main ferryboat system in the area, they peti-
tioned the Indonesian government, and the cups
were banned. Boom! No more plastic cups washing
up. *That's politics.*

People typically see politics as toxic, evil, and ugly.

Like anything in life, they can be those things depending on who is involved.

If we take a broader, more nuanced view, politics in essence are *a means for how we care for one another and the earth*. Put another way, politics are how we negotiate our conflicting visions of what it means to create a life where all can flourish. We are each other's keepers, after all.

Dharma is the very first word in the *Bhagavad Gita*, and it is woven throughout the entire text. The word *dharma* is associated with "duty," but it also means "citizenry," "justice," "goodness," and "decorum." *Dharma* means more than individual responsibility or loyalty to a tribe. It means making a better world for everyone, even your opposition.

I can't tell you how many times when I've posted something about politics (a candidate I'm excited about, a ballot measure I think will help our community, or even just an entreaty for people to vote), I'm met with vitriol in the comments from yoga people lecturing that I should "stick to yoga and leave politics out of it."

When someone finds it distasteful when a yoga teacher posts about politics or brings it into their teaching, their privilege is showing.

The way I see it, and how I was taught by my teachers, is that everything is interconnected — our physical bodies, our breath, our place in the natural world, our biology, and each other.

I was taught that each of us is a microcosm of the macrocosm.

I was taught the Vedic phrase *dehi me, dadami te*, meaning

"give to me, I give to you" — an ancient teaching on the nature of reciprocity and dignity. *Dehi* in Sanskrit is grammatically the second-person imperative of the verb *da*, "to give," suggesting "you should give" / "you will give" / "you ought to give," because life itself puts demands on the living. *Dadami* is the first-person present, "I give," but also hints toward the future, indicating, "I will give."

In contrast to this concept, the world is suffering from excessive individualism and needs desperately for us to give back, not continue relentlessly taking. Despite our inherent interconnectedness, humans have, since the industrial revolution and the move toward city dwellings, become increasingly disconnected from nature and each other — taking more than their share, without giving back to the earth. Considering that you can order a new pair of scissors on Amazon today and it will magically appear at your door by tomorrow, it's evident that humanity is intoxicated with stuff, with little consideration for the energy burned and the toll it took on the earth to bring it to us. This separation from nature stems from the idea that humans have superiority over the environment we live in and depend on rather than being included in, and part of, the natural world.

Yoga was never meant to perpetuate individualism, separation, or superiority over nature. If anything, it encourages union and interdependence with all of creation and the natural world.

Perhaps the greatest example of our interdependence is photosynthesis and respiration — the process of reciprocity that animates the world and gives life to all. Plants convert sunlight into sugar and give life to animals through their breath (oxygen) and the food they provide. Animals in turn give plants carbon dioxide in the form of their breath. It is a life-sustaining, symbiotic relationship.

Given these truths, bringing the world's reality into the yoga classroom is a natural step, and it's imperative if we want to live in harmony with all things and advocate for everyone to be well.

In addition, there will always be incongruity between how the world is and how we'd like it to be. Part of the path of yoga is to contribute to a world we want to see and center ourselves in hope in the midst of what is now a polycrisis.

Now more than ever, as long-held systems that have anchored society seem to be crumbling around us, it is critical that we, as yogins who seek the truth and connection, participate in the world, take part in civic duties like voting, and address society's ills on a local level by cultivating comradery and mutual aid.

As has been said many times, we can't expect to be free and well if others are not yet free or well. In the face of the heightening climate crisis, an all-hands-on-deck, collective effort at mitigation is imperative. Yet engaging citizens who are struggling to put food on the table for their families (and get on board with healing the planet) poses a significant dilemma.

It is urgent that we as individuals start prioritizing collective social well-being and recognizing that we're empowered by our differences, not threatened by them. Then and only then can go about the business of earth care; otherwise we will not have a habitable planet to sustain us. It is my dream to see the yoga world normalize talking about politics and seeing it not as taboo, but as part of what's known as *karma yoga*.

Karma yoga is mentioned frequently in the *Bhagavad*

Gita as one of the three *margas*, or paths of yoga — the other two being *jnana* (knowledge) yoga and *bhakti* (devotion) yoga. The word *karma* comes from the Sanskrit root *kr*, which means "to act." Therefore, karma yoga is the yoga of action and service and is an integral part of the yoga tradition. Indeed, massive action is what is urgently needed in these unprecedented times.

How to Bring the Issues of Our Time into Our Yoga Teaching

"But this is all so dark," you may be saying. "No one wants to feel despair and dread during their yoga practice."

True. However, I believe we can convey the urgency of our time in ways that do not foster doom and gloom but instead inspire resiliency, creativity, hope, and collective action — all qualities to aspire to as a yogin!

Here are some specific ways to bring current events into the classroom without bringing everybody down.

Create Inspiring Class Themes That Apply Yoga to Current Events

Write about what yoga virtues arise when you think of certain difficult current events, and then weave those lessons into a class. For example, if a wildfire burned whole neighborhoods and displaced people in your community, you could take steps like these in class:

- Name the fact that the fire occurred and perhaps share your experience of it and how you're feeling. This shows that you're human and helps model how the students might respond to the tragedy rather than feeling numb or disassociated. You can also invite students to notice how they are feeling.

- In your opening talk, highlight the way certain neighbors and firefighters showed up in the crisis. Did you notice yoga virtues such as courage (*abhaya*) on the part of firefighters or civilians? Heroism (*vīrya*) and compassion (*karuṇā*) from those who rushed into homes to help evacuate trapped pets? Generosity (*dāna*) from those offering their spare bedrooms to evacuees or from businesses that showed up by collecting food, water, and clothing for those who lost everything?

- Shift your focus to one or two of these virtues and how the students can work with them in their practice and in their lives. For example, talk about courage (*abhaya*) in relation to attempting more challenging poses. Or speak about compassion (*karuṇā*) in connection with self-love if modifications are needed in a pose.

- End the class with a contemplation on how each person in the room can commit to making a difference toward climate consciousness and addressing the underlying cause of the fire. Give examples to get them thinking about how they can help, such as supporting local organic farmers if they have the means, commuting by bicycle or public transit instead of by car, unplugging appliances when not in use, not letting their cars idle, supporting climate-conscious businesses, or starting a compost pile.

With all that said, you don't have to bring world events into every class. It's okay to sprinkle in what I call "sanctuary practices" where for the duration of the class you guide the students through awareness — tuning to sensation, theming around the breath, cultivating stillness, or connecting with spirit, for example — in other words, keeping things on the lighter side. In fact, students are craving respite for their over-stimulated nervous systems and managing anxiety (climate anxiety or otherwise). Therefore, intentionally integrating sanctuary practices into your repertoire is important. The key is to strike a balance over time between classes that address the world and classes that are more sanctuary-like. This way, students can trust that you're going to keep it real when it's needed but also offer classes with a "love and light" approach sometimes.

Emphasize Community and Organize Outings

Remember that the number one reason people come back to yoga consistently is community. When times get rough, it's community and comradery that will save us. That said, do not mistake building community in the yoga world for hanging out with others who share a love of yoga pants, fancy props, and the retreat/festival lifestyle. Yoga is much more than that. Yoga is about deepening relationships, having difficult conversations, being in service to something much larger than just yourself, and living an ethical, meaningful life. Community members see one another through birth, death, and everything in between. With so much going on that threatens our very existence, remember that your yoga community can act together to address the issues of our time!

In my own yoga events and classes, I've been actively working on ways to make getting behind causes a community activity that inspires and truly motivates people to become champions for good. At a recent teacher training, instead of going out to dinner like we've done traditionally, we arranged for the group to have a picnic dinner at a local regenerative organic farm, followed by a talk about the farm's nonprofit work regenerating the drylands in our region. The students were given a tour of the land and food forest (agroforestry system) where the founders grow 90 percent of the food they eat.

The evening gave the group three main positive outcomes:

1. It got everyone together breaking bread, bonding, and being in each other's company, which strengthened the sense of community.

2. It educated the group on the importance of creating a livable future, regenerative organic agriculture, and climate consciousness by introducing them to local farmers who are leaders in soil health, carbon sequestration, and food sovereignty in the Boulder, Colorado, area. Boulder is known to be dry and fire prone, and its soil is threatened by desertification, so the students became aware of the local environmental issues.

3. It gave the students the opportunity to take action themselves. Some of our local students went on to become regular volunteers for the farm and nonprofit!

This is just one example of many activities that can bring people off their yoga mats and involve them in the very real challenges faced by many in their local areas — not just environmental but also social.

Here are some ideas for group activities outside your yoga classes that you could add as *seva* trips:

- A group beach cleanup
- A potluck dinner followed by a documentary screening (Netflix has loads of documentaries on social and environmental awareness)
- A group outing to a special educational museum exhibit
- A nature walk or boat ride with a naturalist
- A farm tour during the growing season
- An organic farm-to-table dinner in collaboration with local chefs and farmers to foster community and raise awareness on the importance of regenerative organic agriculture — the price of admission can cover the cost of the chef and the food grown by the farmers
- A monthly book club around cause-driven books or books by Black and Brown authors

Create an Environmentally Friendly Yoga Space

If you own a studio or run a yoga event, create systems that promote environmental stewardship. This could include:

- Promoting composting and recycling by having labeled waste bins for compost, recycling, and landfill trash
- Eliminating single-use plastic from the space. If you sell water and other drinks, source those in glass bottles or aluminum cans, and ask students not to bring in single-use plastics of their own
- Making the studio a zero-waste facility by, for example, laundering hand towels for the bathrooms
- Using biodegradable cleaners and hand soap rather than commercial cleaning products
- Conserving energy by putting your thermostats on a

schedule and not heating the studio space above normal room temperature

- Unplugging unnecessary appliances and electronics when not in use

Create a Culture of Belonging

Representation matters in facilitating a welcoming, accessible space for all. If you operate a yoga studio or are producing a yoga event, make sure you hire a well-rounded team that includes a diverse representation of yoga teachers, staff, managers, and producers.

In addition, consider representation in your promotional materials. Are the images all of thin white women? Make an effort to photograph or use stock images of folks of different ages, races, body sizes, and gender identities.

Consider creating a DEI (diversity, equity, and inclusion) statement for your studio or event. Having a DEI statement requires a lot of inner work and then sends a message to a broad group of potential students that your studio or event is a welcoming space for them. In addition, it will exhibit how you engage in DEI efforts through your classes and reveal opportunities for collaboration (with individuals and organizations) that you might want to explore more.

Normalize Civic and Political Engagement

If we talk about civic engagement and politics in terms of collective care and building a better world, we can start to normalize them as something we might unite behind as opposed to being about toxic division and ugliness. Linking these ideas to yoga teachings (such as dharma) is an especially effective approach.

Foster Mutual Aid in Your Yoga Community

The Covid-19 pandemic and the increase of climate disasters, economic uncertainty, and racist violence have made the idea of mutual aid more and more well known. Mutual aid is when everyday people come together to meet each other's needs when the systems they rely on are no longer meeting those needs. It does not necessarily mean that people should stop pressuring power structures to take care of their citizens; rather, it's the idea that people can meet each other's needs together, immediately, when the government can't or won't. Examples of mutual aid include neighborhood pods composed of people who can rely on each other for support; collective donation funds; and food drives for those in need. Local yoga studios can be hubs for helping the community organize mutual aid projects.

―――――――――

In conclusion, we believe that yoga teachers are leaders in our society. We believe if yoga teachers give themselves permission to be more involved in their communities, participate more in civics, and be courageous enough to bring the challenges we face as a humanity into the yoga practice and inspire students to do the same, we can collectively be among the changemakers who will build a better world.

Light Up the World

To be a yoga teacher is to embody what it means to have well-being in life, and in turn to impart that understanding to others. Teaching yoga is a sacred calling for many. Indeed, it is one of the most rewarding professions out there — not many others can say that it's their job to make people feel good!

Much of this book has been about how to skillfully serve, inspire, and assist yoga students. Yet perhaps the most rewarding part of this profession is the one that centers on ourselves. Being a yoga teacher grants each of us the opportunity to be a lifelong student and create a more meaningful life for ourselves. It's a career that has self-care, self-inquiry, and self-discovery built right into the job description. The perks are seemingly endless: enhanced self-awareness, learning, community, and a personal yoga practice that supports our body, heart, and mind for years to come.

Ironically, the more we "selfishly" benefit from yoga and a career in yoga, the more we excel in our teaching and as a result mobilize our students to shift their own lives for the better. Ultimately, we study yoga and train in yoga to know ourselves more deeply, and when we radiate that self-awareness is when we shine brightest as teachers. One thing I know for sure is that great yoga teachers make the world a more peaceful, intelligent, and conscious place to be.

Refer to these pages for inspiration often. Take action on the ideas that resonate most. Keep studying the vast infinitude that is yoga philosophy, asana, pranayama, and meditation. Study anatomy and biomechanics. And be a lifelong student of business and marketing so that your yoga has the proper vehicle to get out into the world!

Trust yourself and your own authentic seat as the teacher. Carve out and claim the time to care for yourself, do your practice, and kindle your own fire. Then watch how your enthusiasm and energy can light up another's life. This is how we help wake up the world.

Acknowledgments

We are profoundly grateful for the teachings of Douglas Brooks, PhD, who Amy has had the privilege of studying with since 1999. His wisdom, friendship, research in ancient languages, pilgrimages throughout India, and teachings from his teacher, Gopala Aiyar Sundaramoorthy, have greatly influenced our understanding of the yoga philosophy shared throughout this book.

We are also deeply appreciative of the following people for their contributions, encouragement, support, and inspiration: Jennifer Ippoliti, Roberta Beech, Dick Ippoliti, Raymond Beech, Haruko Smith, Manorama Thea D'Alvia, Sara Ivanhoe, Elena Brower, Julie Holly, Anne Libby, Dana Flynn, Judith Lasater, PhD, Cyndi Lee, Jack Canfield, Marie Forleo, Jim Bunch, Nia Desiré Clark, MSW, Monika Fleshner, PhD, David Jacobs, Ron Katz, Chiara Pennella, Reggie Hubbard, Amy Stanton, Georgia Hughes, Kristen Cashman, Keith Martin Smith, Jeff Tkach, Jeff Moyer, Annie Brown, Sue Elkind, and Yoshi Aono. To our late grandmothers, Ernestine Perrie (Nonnie) and Mitsue Kubota (Omama) — we love you, we thank you, we miss you.

We are also grateful to every yoga teacher we have had the opportunity to train — without your questions, vulnerability, and courage, writing this book would not have been possible.

Index

abdominal work, 186
abhaya, 265
accountants, 166
accounting skills, 47, 108
administrative skills, 47
Advaita Vedanta, 12
advance revenue, 78, 83
Affordable Care Act, 168
Alchemical Body, The (White), 15
algorithms: email as free from, 138;
     political polarization and, 253;
     social media engagement and,
     141, 144, 147, 150, 152
alignment: anatomical, instructions
     based on, 177; -based yoga, 18,
     200, 218; observation teaching
     and, 218; online classes and, 217;
     teacher assistance with problems
     of, 42, 91, 102, 131; skilled teach-
     ing of, 200, 202; standing poses
     and teaching of, 186; teacher
     training in, 17–18, 22; vinyasa
     yoga and, 216
alignment techniques, 131, 186
Alo, 70
anecdotes, 176, 182, 184, 188, 203, 213
ankle-to-knee pose, 225
anxiety, 252, 266
apex poses, 183, 185, 187, 192
appearance, physical, 247–48

applications (apps), 69, 154–55
ardha chandrasana, 192
ardha matsyendrasana, 178
arm balances, 186, 206
artificial intelligence (AI), 232. *See also*
     ChatGPT
arts, as theme source, 192
asana practice, 1, 19, 148, 272. *See also*
     poses; sequences
asana setup in online teaching, 97–98
asynchronous teachings, 74, 80, 84, 85
athletes, 49, 50, 52, 65
attention span, 220, 222, 228, 253–54
auchitya, 26–27
audio, 90, 94, 99–101, 150, 154, 214
auditions, 109, 176–77
authenticity: charisma and, 28;
     ChatGPT and, 235–36; core
     values and, 34–36; exemplary
     yoga teachers and, 23–24;
     marketing and, 124, 126; online
     yoga and, 221, 227; social media
     and, 157–58; substandard yoga
     teachers and, 29; yoga-speak and,
     204–5; "yoga voice" and, 221
Autobiography (Franklin), 37
awareness, 266

bank accounts, 166
beauty, 31

Beck, Martha, 28
beginner series/classes: author's experience, 49; balanced schedule including, 61, 62; income from, 49–50; marketing funnel and, 125–26; online, 226; promotions for, 63; rewards of, 48–49; rural teaching and, 113; scheduling, 117
Bhagavad Gita, 261, 263–64
bhakti yoga, 264
bias, unconscious, 254–55
bind in revolved extended side angle, 225
bios, 143
blended learning. *See* hybrid learning
blogs, 56, 233
Bluetooth, 100
body language, 28
bolsters, 215
bookkeepers, 166
books, as theme source, 192
Boulder (CO), 49, 132, 168–69, 267
boundaries, 51–52, 166
brain fog, 253–54
branding, 126–28
breakout rooms, 74
breathwork, 57, 191. *See also* pranayama
brevity, 143–44
broadband connection, 89–90
Brooks, Douglas, 126
budgeting, 166
Bunch, Jim, 36
business and yoga, 16, 123
business building, xii; business plan, 107–8; ChatGPT and, 232–33; day jobs and, 113–14; resumé, 108–9; in rural areas, 113; studio-opening decisions, 120–22; sustainable teaching and, 114–20; teaching opportunities, 109–12
business cards, 125, 135
business channels: balancing, 60–63; decision-making for, 59–60; identifying, 47; online yoga, 75–93; partnerships/endorsements, 32, 56, 151–52; product sales, 55; student base development for, 63–68; workplace/school classes, 56–58, 184. *See also* beginner

series/classes; conferences; group classes; online yoga; private lessons; retreats; specialty series/workshops; teacher training; workshops
business entity setup, 166
business finances: basic management strategies, 165–67; charitable contributions, 169–70; insurance, 167–69; as teaching "container" component, 241
business plan, 39, 107–8
business skills, 47

California Yoga Teachers Association Code of Conduct, 25
cameras, 89–90, 95–97, 102–3, 216
candles, 99
Canfield, Jack, 36
centering, 186, 198, 201
certifications, 108–9
chakras, 191–92
charisma, 27–28, 200
charitable contributions, 169–70, 241, 270
ChatGPT: defined, 232; prompts on, 234–35; responsible use of, 235–36; shortcomings of, 233–34; student cheating with, 237–38; yoga-related uses of, 232–33, 235–38
children, 52, 161
civic engagement, 269
classes: alignment-based, 218; attendance at, 4, 60, 110; author's experience, 1; balanced schedule for, 60–63; ChatGPT and, 233; community-related group activities outside of, 267–68; current events in, 264–70; as escape, 258–60, 264; free, 11–12; hands-on assists during, 182; in-person, and Covid-19 pandemic, 70, 72; inspirational message at start of, 176, 199–200, 209 (*see also* dharma talks); length of, 184; location of, 115–16; missing, 118, 205–6; multilevel, 206–8; online drop-in, 77–79, 83; pacing of, 182, 183, 199–200; as refuge, 19;

relationship with, 159; size of, 111, 118–19; structure in, 180–81; student expectations of, 41, 42–43, 54; at studios, 110–12; successful yoga teachers and, 29–30; theme-free, 196; time management in, 23, 51–52, 201; time of, 60; types of, 47–48; at workplaces/schools, 56–58. *See also* beginner series/classes; class planning/preparation; conferences; group classes; hybrid classes; in-person classes, skillful teaching of; online yoga; online yoga, skillful teaching of; private lessons; retreats; specialty series/workshops; teacher training; workshops

class planning/preparation: balanced amount of, 180–81; challenges of, 173; "container" for, 173, 241–42; importance of, 173, 201–2, 212–14; for online classes, 103–6; 212–14; "packing list" for, 174; repetition in, 177, 187; teaching binder for, 174–80, 196; template for, 182–87; theme usage, 188–96

clients, dissatisfied, 155

climate crisis, 252, 263, 266, 270

clothing, 110, 111

code of conduct, 25

coffee shops, 64, 125, 133, 135

colleagues, relationships with, 159, 162–64

commenting on social media, 144

commercialization, 10

communication, 139, 163, 254

community: class scheduling and, 117; as core value, 36–37; emphasizing, in yoga teaching, 266–68; group classes and, 50; online classes and, xi, 222, 226–27; relationships with, 4, 9, 159; retreats and, 54, 161; rural teaching and, 113; *seva* and, 170; social media and, 139, 140, 141; successful yoga teachers and, 29; teachers' yoga practice and, 246

community wellness publications, 135

compassion, xi, 265

conciseness, 201, 213, 217, 219, 220, 222

conferences: attendance at, as marketing strategy, 135–36; marketing of, 12; student attendance at, 130; as yoga business channel, 48, 54–55

confidence, 181

connection, 24; AI and, 236–37; author's experience, 148, 161; online yoga and building of, 227–28; professional, 31; *seva* and, 170; social media and, 139, 141, 148, 157; social networking and, 137; student expectations for, 42–43; teacher-student relationship and, 68, 139, 140; as theme source, 224; yoga classes as sites of, 19; yoga pedigree and, 32–33; as yoga philosophy element, 137, 162, 263. *See also* interdependence

consistency, 143

consumerism, 15, 55

content, 140–41, 144

cool-downs, 209

core work, 186

corporate yoga, 56–58, 184

courage, 265

Coursera.com, 142

Covid-19 pandemic: isolation during, 254; mutual aid and, 270; online yoga and, xi, 70–72, 89, 215; professionalism and, 224; subscription model and, 76; teacher home practice during, 243; yoga prop improvisation during, 215; yoga studios and, 230

creativity, 244–45

critical thinking, 236, 237–38, 254

criticism, 34–35. *See also* feedback

cross-promotion, 153–54

Crunch Fitness (New York, NY), 161

curating, 140, 142, 144, 147, 150

curiosity, 162

current events: ChatGPT and, 234; politics and, 260–61; social/environmental problems, xi, 251–53, 260; as theme source, 194, 264–66; yoga classes and avoidance of, 258–61; in yoga teaching, 264–70; yoga world as impacted by, 253–55

curriculum, 80, 81, 85
customer care, 66–67, 80–81, 83

dakshina, 13
dāna, 265
darshan, 72
date nights, 161
day jobs, 59, 113–14
decluttering, 248–49
dehi me, dadami te, 261–62
DEI statements, 269
demonstration teaching, 97–98; 215–17
demos, 202, 203, 209
dependability, 112
devotion, 264
dharana, 173, 241
dharma, 261, 269
dharma talks: conciseness in, 209, 213, 221, 228; online filming setup for, 97; rehearsing, 213; skillful teaching and, 199–200; subject ideas for, 236; as yoga class component, 176
diet, 248
digital fatigue, 72
digital void, 222–23, 227
digital yoga. See online yoga
direct messages (DMs), 144
discipline, 30
disclaimers, 206–7
discussion boards, 74
distractions, 94, 100–101, 224, 253–54
diversity, 269
divine, the: breath as link between the physical and, 191; as energy source, 39, 197; openness to direction from, 197–98; relationship with, 159, 160
drishti, 227–28
Duet videos, 152, 154

e-commerce systems, 76–77, 79, 82, 84, 90
economic uncertainty, xi
e-courses. See online courses
education: continuing, 4, 61–62, 108; multifaceted, yoga as, 13; résumés

detailing, 108–9; social media and, 153
ego, 39
eight limbs of yoga, 25
email, 88, 113, 125, 133, 135
emotional health, 246–47
endorsement deals, 32, 56, 151–52
engagement, 144, 147, 154
enthusiasm, 162, 244–45
environmental issues, xi, 9, 252–53, 260
equity, 269
ethics, 10–11, 24–27. See also values
exercise, physical, 247–248
exercises: brand creation, 126–128; core values list, 35–37; how to use, 4; ideal student identification, 41–43, 129–31; mission statement, 39–40; reasons for teaching, 37–39
eye contact, 28, 201, 202–3, 227–28

Facebook: algorithm of, 144, 147; author's experience, 127, 147–48; business building on, 56, 65, 113; current popularity of, 137; event pages on, 146–47; friends on, 147; marketing funnel and, 125–26; marketing on, 127, 134, 147; microblogging on, 143–44; personal profile pages on, 145–46; "population" of, 139; professional business pages on, 145, 146; tips for using, 146–47; yoga students' use of, 141
facial expressions, 211, 212, 223
fads, 30
family: online cameo appearances of, 224; relationships with, 159, 160–61
fashion sense, 32
feedback: class planning/preparation and, 175, 200–201; for core value identification, 35–37; critical, 34–35; leadership and, 27; online yoga and, 89, 97, 101, 217, 218, 226, 229, 231; on promotional material, 124; relationship-building and, 163; social media and,

155–57; from students, 110, 111–12, 205, 211, 226
fierce pose, 209
film, as theme source, 192
financial backing, 107
financial team, 166
fitness classes, 162, 176
flat fees, 51, 58
Floyd, George, 254
flyers, 125, 133, 139
Flynn, Dana Trixie, 242, 244–45
food drives, 270
Franklin, Benjamin, 37
friendliness, 163
friends: feedback from, 200–201; relationships with, 159, 160–61
"fruit-salad" schedule, 119–20
fundraisers, 62, 168

gender, 31–32
generosity, 162, 265
Gen Z, 139
gift certificates, 63
Glo, 70, 87, 127
goals, 30, 39, 111, 124
"go-givers" vs. "go-getters," 164
Google, 193
Google Bard, 232, 234
Google Hangouts, 89, 91
graciousness, 164
gratitude, 164, 193
gratitude journals, 160
grief, 194–95
grounding, 189
group classes: balanced schedule including, 60, 62; income from, 50–51; marketing funnel and, 125–26; notes about, 179; rewards of, 50; successful yoga teachers and, 29
guest teaching, 109, 110, 205–6
gunas, 176

habits, cultivating new, 205
half-moon pose, 192
"hallucinations," AI, 233–34
hands-on assists, xi, 89, 182, 202, 204
handstands, 80, 206
hashtags, 148, 149, 150, 154

haters, 155, 156–57
health-care costs, 124, 252
health food stores, 135
health insurance, 167–68
helpfulness, 162
heroism, 265
Hindu deities, 190
holding poses, 209
holidays, as theme source, 193
home yoga practice, 243–44
Horan, Jim, 107
hot yoga, 30, 200
hourly rates, 51
humility, 27, 39, 170
humor, 222–23, 227
hybrid classes: defined, 73; fads in, 30; online drop-in classes and, 77–78; online series and, 82; online teacher training and, 84; teaching guidelines, 230–31; at yoga studios, 91, 92, 230–31
hybrid learning, 74–75, 92, 218
hydraulic verbs, 180
hygiene, personal, 248

inclusion, 269
income: from beginner series/classes, 49–50; from group classes, 51; from partnerships/endorsements, 56; passive, 80; from private lessons, 51, 58; from product sales, 55; from retreats, 54; success and, 29–30; from teacher trainings, 51, 53–54; from workplace/school classes, 58
India, yoga history in, 12, 13
individualism, 262
infotainment, 152–53
injuries: ChatGPT and, 233; liability lawsuits and, 168–69; multilevel classes and, 206; online yoga and risk of, 217, 218; specialty series addressing, 50; student fears of, 131; students with, 42, 212; teacher-student relationship and, 161; "vicious cycle" of yoga teaching and, 16
injury prevention, 18, 65
inner quieting, 255–56

in-person classes, skillful teaching of:
    divine direction in, 197–98; mul-
    tilevel classes and, 206–8; online
    teaching vs., 211–12; pacing for,
    199–200; partner work and,
    203–4; positive habits, 201–3;
    presence and, 200; relating to
    students, 200–205; substitute
    teachers and, 205–6; time man-
    agement, 208–9
inspiration, chance, 193
Instagram: author's experience,
    156; business building on, 56;
    ChatGPT and, 233; current
    popularity of, 137; Discover
    Page on, 150; feed planner apps
    on, 150; marketing on, 127, 134;
    microblogging on, 143–44; photo
    curation on, 142; photos on,
    148; "population" of, 139; Reels,
    149–50, 233; Stories, 150–51; tips
    for using, 149–51; yoga business
    uses of, 148–49; yoga students'
    use of, 141; yogin fame on, 151–52
instruction notes, 177–78
insurance, 167–69
interdependence, 40, 256–57, 261–63
introductions, 214, 221
introductory trial offers, 79
inversions, 186, 209
Iyengar, B.K.S., 32

Jackson, Michael, 197–98
jargon, 203, 204–5
Jivamukti Yoga Center, 161
jnana yoga, 264
Jois, Pattabhi, 32
journaling, 160, 188, 246–47

Kajabi, 75, 82
kalapurnata, 256–57
karma, 25, 26, 27, 264
karma yoga, xii, 263–64
Kartra, 75, 82
karunā, 265
keywords, 150
kindness, 162
King, Martin Luther, Jr., 257

kirtan musicians, 199
knowledge, 264
koshas, 176
Krishna Das, 161, 199
kundalini, 249

Laughing Lotus Yoga Center, 244–45
lawsuits, 168–69
leadership, 27
learning management software (LMS),
    75, 82
lecture setup, 97
Lee, Cyndi, 1
leisure time, 115
LGBTQIA+ community, 255
liability: insurance, 167, 168–69;
    release forms, 169
life challenges: as theme source,
    194–96
lighting, 90, 93–95, 98–99
light theme, 180
likes, 144, 146
lila, 25–26, 27
limbs of yoga, 25
limitations, 42
LinkedIn, 108, 137, 145
listening skills, 29
live cohorts, 81
livestream yoga classes: breakout
    rooms, 223; Covid-19 pandemic
    and, 70; defined, 73; demonstra-
    tion teaching in, 215–17; hybrid
    classes and, 73; meeting software
    for, 79, 84; observation teach-
    ing in, 101, 215, 217–19; online
    courses and, 74, 77; online series
    and, 82; production/setup for,
    94–95, 97, 100; pros/cons of, 212,
    224; skilled teaching practices,
    221–27; student setup for, 101,
    102–3; studios offering, 91
loans, 107
love, 193
loyalty, 67–68

Madonna, 2
manners, 162
mantra repetition, 160, 198, 221

margas, 264
marketing: author's experience, 16,
127, 128; beginning students and,
125–26; branding for, 126–28;
ChatGPT and, 233; of confer-
ence classes, 55; confidence with,
124–25; example sites for, 125; five
Ps of, 131–32; getting to enjoy,
129; gift certificates, 63; goal
identification for, 124; importance of, 13–14, 122, 123–24; offline strategies, 135–36; for online
courses, 81, 82, 225–26; for online
series, 84; for online teacher
training, 87; plan for, 60, 132–34;
scheduling for, 134; sleazy, 13;
social media and, 139, 144; studio
teaching and, 51, 53; successful
yoga teachers and acumen for,
32; target market identification,
128–31; of yoga accessories, 12,
56; of yoga retreats, 47; yogin
aversion to, 10–11, 122, 123
marketing funnel, 125–26
marketing plans: creating, 60, 132–34;
for online workshops, 79
market research, 83
massage therapists, 18, 109
materialism, 123
mats, 1, 7, 94, 102–3
meditation: as asana class component, 187; author's experience,
160; business building and, 59;
distractions during, 55; on the
divine, 198; lifelong practice of,
272; online filming setup for, 99,
100; popularity of, 71; preclass,
224; *purusha* and, 14–15; social
media and, 153; spiritual bypassing and, 259; workplace yoga
teaching and, 57; yoga and, 7
meditation journal, 244
meetings, online video, 73, 118, 215
meetups, 81
membership hosting services, 76–77
Member-Vault, 77
men: as yoga students, 52; as yoga
teachers, 31–32

mental health, 246–47
microblogging, 143–44, 154–55
microphones, 100
Microsoft Bing, 232, 234
Millennials, 139
mindfulness, 7
mini-vinyasa flows, 179
mission statement, 37, 39–40, 108, 175,
198, 241
modifications, 207, 212, 213–14, 265
money: troubles with, 165; yoga and,
16, 123. *See also* business finances
monotone, 221
multilevel classes, 206–8
music, 30, 182, 193
muting/unmuting, 214
mutual aid, 270
mystique, 30

Namastream, 77
natural cycle themes, 190
nature, disconnection from, 262
neighborhood pods, 270
nervousness, 136
networking, in-person, 136. *See also*
social networking
newsletters, 133, 139, 233
niche audiences, 87
niche subjects, 52, 80
"90 Minutes to Change the World"
course, 3–4, 15, 119–20, 129, 131
90 Monkeys, 3, 35. *See also* Vesselify
niyamas, 24–27, 176
nursing, 109

Obamacare, 168
observation teaching, 101, 215, 217–19
O'Connor, Sinéad, 257
OfferingTree, 77
on-demand videos: author's experience, 70, 220; class planning/
preparation, 81–82; defined, 73;
online courses and, 74, 77; pro-
duction/setup for, 94–95, 96, 100;
pros/cons of, 80, 212, 227; skillful
teaching of, 214, 227–30; studios
offering, 91, 227; for teacher
trainings, 86, 87

One Page Business Plan, The (Horan),
     107
online courses, 74, 80–82
online fitness platforms, 87–88
online libraries, 79
online networking sites, 108
online platforms, 82
online relationships, 159
online video meetings, 73
online yoga: class preparation for,
     103–6; 212–14; courses, 74,
     80–82; Covid-19 pandemic
     and, xi, 70–72, 89, 215; defined,
     69; drop-in classes/workshops,
     77–79, 83; history of, 69–70;
     hybrid classes, 91–92; platforms,
     87–88; private lessons, 89–91;
     production equipment/setup for,
     93–101; pros/cons of, 70–72, 75,
     100; self-marketing in, 225–26;
     specialty series, 82–84; student
     setup for, 101–3; subscription
     model, 75–77, 82; teacher train-
     ings, 84–87; terminology, 72–75;
     yoga/fitness platforms, 87–88;
     YouTube classes, 92–93. *See also*
     hybrid classes; livestream yoga
     classes; on-demand videos; on-
     line yoga, skillful teaching of
online yoga, skillful teaching of, xii;
     class planning/preparation,
     103–6; 212–14; demonstration vs.
     observation teaching of, 215–19;
     in-person teaching vs., xi, 211–12;
     of livestream classes, 215–19, 221–
     27; of on-demand content, 214,
     227–30; props for, 215; student
     engagement/retention, 219–21
organization, personal, 248–49
Origins of Yoga and Tantra, The
     (Samuel), 15
overhead costs, 11–12
overthinking, 198

pain relief, 49
pandemics, 252. *See also* Covid-19
     pandemic
parents, new, 64, 118

Parker, Gail, 255–56
parking, 116
partner classes, 204
partnerships, 32, 56
partner work, 203–4
passive income, 80
Patanjali, 12, 14–15, 24, 25
Patreon, 70, 77
PayPal, 79, 90
Peloton, 87
personal development, 115
perspiration, 211, 212
philanthropy, 169–70
philosophy, yoga: AI and, 236; class-
     work with, 175, 182, 185, 188–89,
     190; *dharma* in, 261; interdepen-
     dence in, 261–62; karma yoga,
     xii, 263–64; lifelong study of,
     272; material world as viewed
     in, 14–15, 123; online lectures on,
     71; social networking and, 137;
     teacher training in, 18; time as
     viewed in, 256–57
photic verbs, 180
photosynthesis, 262–63
physical focus, 182, 185
physical prowess, 31
physical therapists, 18, 109
pigeon pose, 225
Pinterest, 154
place, 132, 133
plastic pollution, 252–53, 260
polarization, 253
police violence, 251, 254
politics, 260–61, 269
pollution, 252–53, 260
poses: ankle-to-knee, 225; apex, 183,
     185, 187, 192; ardha chandrasana,
     192; ardha matsyendrasana, 178;
     fierce, 209; half-moon, 192; hand-
     stands, 80, 206; holding, 209;
     pigeon, 225; preparatory, 186;
     revolved extended side angle,
     225; scorpion, 206; seated, 225;
     standing, 186, 191; supta padan-
     gustasana, 208; triangle, 208
position, marketing, 132, 133
postcards, 125, 135

posture, 28, 191
prakriti, 14, 15
pranayama, 71, 153, 198, 272. *See also*
   breathwork
preparatory poses, 186
presence, 200
present moment, the, 256
price, 132, 133
private lessons: balanced schedule
   including, 60, 62; building
   student base for, 51–52; business
   skills required for, 47; hands-on
   assists during, 89; income from,
   51, 58, 114; marketing funnel and,
   125–26; notes about, 179; online,
   89–91, 218; promotions for, 63;
   scheduling, 118; successful yoga
   teachers and, 29
proactivity, 112
product, 131, 133
product sales, 55
professional connections, 31
professionalism, 110, 111, 224
promotion, 132, 133, 144, 153–54, 269.
   See also marketing
prompt engineering, AI, 234–35
props, 183, 185–86, 213, 214, 215
psychographics, 129
psychotherapy, 109
pulsation, 180, 189–90
punch cards, 78, 79
Punchpass, 79, 90
punctuality, 112, 208–9, 226
purusha, 14–15

Qualman, Eric, 138–39
questionnaires, 42, 129–30
quotes, 179

racism, 251, 254, 270
reciprocity, 262–63
referrals, 135
Registered Yoga Teacher credentials,
   109
rehearsals, 213, 214
relationship-building: importance of,
   159–60, 241; online classes and,
   212; personal, 32, 39, 160–61, 241,

246, 247; private lessons and, 47;
   professional, 110, 111–12, 161–64,
   241; self-care and, 246, 247; social
   networking and, 137; studio
   teaching jobs and, 88, 112, 120;
   as teaching "container" component, 241; types of, 159; as yoga
   career skill, 4; as yoga value, 2,
   137, 266. *See also* teacher-student
   relationship
rental expenses, 54
repetition, 177, 187, 203
reputation, 55
respiration, 262–63
restorative yoga, 71
*Restorative Yoga for Ethnic and
   Race-Based Stress and Trauma*
   (Parker), 255–56
résumés, 108–9, 145
retreats: author's experience, 161; balanced schedule including, 60, 61,
   62; business skills required for,
   47, 54; ChatGPT and, 233; income
   from, 54; marketing funnel and,
   125–26; online teacher trainings
   and, 84; partner work in, 204;
   teacher-student relationship
   during, 161
revolved extended side angle pose, 225
role models, 22, 23, 48, 242
root chakra, 192

sales calls, 87
Samuel, Geoffrey, 15
sanctuary practices, 265–66
satya, 236
savasana, 187, 193, 203, 209
savings, 167
scheduling, 59; apps for, 154; author's
   experience, 2, 132; balanced/sus-
   tainable, 60–62, 114–15, 116–20,
   241; environmental conservation and, 268–69; "fruit salad,"
   119–20; life challenges and,
   195; marketing and, 132–34, 134;
   online yoga and, 71, 77, 78, 83, 91,
   228, 230; relationship-building
   and, 161, 247; self-care and, 198;

scheduling (*continued*)
    social media and, 134, 143, 154;
    studio teaching jobs and, 91, 112,
    184; successful yoga teachers
    and, 29; teacher practice time
    included in, 17, 245; yoga series
    and, 49
schools, yoga classes at, 58
scorpion pose, 206
search engine optimization (SEO), 150
seated poses, 225
self, relationship with, 159, 160
self-assessment, 21
self-assists, 214, 224–25
self-awareness, 9–10, 21, 236, 271–72
self-care, 160, 271; importance of,
    242; mental/emotional health,
    246–47; organization, 248–49;
    physical appearance and
    well-being, 247–48; as teaching
    "container" component, 241–42;
    yoga practice as, 242–46
self-doubt, 29
self-esteem, 9–10, 169–70
self-inquiry, 21, 255–56, 271
self-love, 193
self-paced learning, 74
self-presentation, 34, 155–58
self-promotion, 122, 225
self-reflection, 39
self-talk, 29
sensitivity, 162
sequences: author's experience,
    177; ChatGPT and, 233; class
    planning/preparation for, 173,
    176, 177, 180–87; describing, 180;
    modifications to, 207, 212, 213–14,
    265; multilevel classes and, 208;
    in online classes, 213–14; stan-
    dard elements of, 186–87; teacher
    training for, 17–18; template
    for, 182–86; verbs used for, 180;
    vinyasa flows within, 179
service, xi–xii, 169–70, 263–64, 266
seva, 169–70, 267–68
sharing, 144–45
"Shit Unprofessional Yoga Teachers
    Say" video, 35

"Shit Yoga Teachers Say," 204–5
shot lists, 233
shyness, 147–48
size, people of, 255
skillful teaching. *See* in-person classes,
    skillful teaching of; online yoga,
    skillful teaching of
skills, 37, 109
slide presentations, 214
smartphones, 97, 253–54
smiling, 223–24, 227–28
Smith, Taro, 3–4
social contract, 27
social issues, xi, 9
socializing, 212
social media: addiction to, 138;
    author's experience, 156; aversion
    to, 140; basic guidelines for,
    142–45; ChatGPT and, 233;
    distractive nature of, 160, 253–54;
    four Cs of, 140–42; haters on,
    155, 156–57; interactive nature
    of, 155; marketing on, 125; old-
    school alternatives to, 135–36;
    online courses for using, 142;
    online yoga platforms and, 88;
    popular platforms, 137, 145–55;
    professional posts on, 155–58;
    reasons to embrace, 138–39; yoga
    teachers and, 138–39. *See also*
    specific platform
social networking: aversion to, 138,
    140; fun with, 145; old-school
    alternatives to, 135–36; reasons to
    embrace, 138–39; skills for, 32, 56,
    142; yoga philosophy and, 137
Socialnomics (Qualman), 138–39
social problems, 251–53
sonic verbs, 180
spaciousness, 202
spanda, 189
specialty series/workshops: balanced
    schedule including, 60, 61, 62;
    marketing funnel and, 126; on-
    line, 82–84; possible themes for,
    52; promotions for, 63; as yoga
    business channel, 48, 50
spiritual bypassing, 26, 258–60

spiritual practice, 7
sports medicine, 18
stability, 25–26, 27
staff, relationship with, 159, 162–64
standing poses, 186, 191
Stein, Ben, 160
still images, 142
Sting, 2
Stitch videos, 154
stress, 165
stress relief, 49, 123
students: accountability of, 217,
    219, 220–21; acquiring, 66–67;
    affluent, 114; AI and cheating
    by, 237–38; attention span of,
    220, 222, 228; beginners, 48–49,
    125–26; building base of, 34, 51,
    63–68; connecting with, 41–42,
    141, 148; dissatisfied, 220–21;
    drop-off among, 213; elderly,
    49; expectations of, 41, 42–43,
    54; ideal, identifying, 41–43,
    63–66, 124, 128–31; inspiring, 4;
    international, online platforms
    and, 87–88; listening to, 29; loyal,
    67–68; notes about, 179; online
    classes and, 101–3, 216–21; part-
    ner work and, 203–4; referrals
    from, 135; relationship with, 159;
    retaining, 67, 213, 219–21; skilled
    teachers and, 200–205; social
    media and, 139, 141; sounds made
    by, 211–12; "spotlighting," 218; val-
    ues of, 9. See also teacher-student
    relationship
studios: ChatGPT and, 232–33; class
    length at, 184; Covid-19 pan-
    demic and, 70; DEI statement
    for, 269; environmentally friendly,
    268–68; as exclusive spaces,
    254–55; getting hired at, 109–10;
    location of, 115–16; mutual aid
    projects at, 270; online classes
    offered by, 91–93; online teacher
    trainings and, 84; opening one's
    own, 120–22; overhead costs at,
    166; payment models at, 51, 116;
    professional relationships in, 159,
    162–64; pros/cons of teaching
    at, 91–92, 115–20; scheduling
    at, 110–12; social functions
    in, 162–63, 212; social media
    and, 149; student base at, 116;
    teachers' yoga practice at, 245; in
    urban areas, 114; values/goals of,
    109, 112
subscription model, 75–77, 82
substitute teaching: arranging for, 112,
    195–96, 205–6; life challenges
    and, 195–96; scheduling prob-
    lems and, 118; teaching opportu-
    nities through, 109–10
supta padangustasana, 208
syllabi, 80
symbiosis, 262–63
synchronous teachings, 74, 80, 84

tablets, 97
talents, 38, 39
Tantra, 15
Tao Te Ching, 1
Tarkeshi, Jasmine, 244
tax advisers, 166
taxes, 108
Teachable, 75, 77, 82
teachers: author's experience, 1, 31,
    200; career skills, 4; ChatGPT
    and, 232–33; as community lead-
    ers, 270; continuing education
    for, 4, 61–62; Covid-19 pandemic
    and, 70; credentials of, 108–9; ex-
    emplary, 21–22, 23–28, 67; fitness
    of, 216; improvement areas for,
    33, 40; income sources for,
    47, 114 (*see also* business chan-
    nels); international, online study
    with, 71; liability lawsuits against,
    168–69; life challenges and,
    194–96; mission statement for,
    37, 39–40, 198; "pedigreed,"
    32–33; personal stories of, 176,
    190–91; professional relation-
    ships of, 159–64; reasons for
    becoming, 37–39, 40; reputation
    of, 55, 162; self-assessment of,
    21–22; skilled, 21–23, 67 (*see also*
    in-person classes, skillful

teachers (*continued*)
  teaching of; online yoga, skillful
    teaching of); social media and,
    138–39; spiritual bypassing by,
    258–60; substandard, 23, 26,
    28–29, 203; successful, 21–22,
    29–33; values of, 33–37, 40; voice
    quality of, 221; yoga practice of,
    242–46. *See also* teacher-student
    relationship; teacher training
teacher-student relationship, 159;
  abuses of, 55; author's experience,
  161; ethics and, 24–25; history of,
  13; skilled teachers and, 200–205
teacher training: aspects of, 52;
  author's experience, 15–16; challenges of, 52–53; ChatGPT and,
  236–38; demand for, 10; duration
  of, 18; ethics and, 24–25; income
  from, 51, 53–54; marketing funnel
  and, 126; online, 69–70, 84–87,
  218; professional development,
  69–70; recommended topics in,
  17–18; spiritual bypassing in,
  259–60; theme usage and, 188
teaching binder: anecdotes/contem-
  plations in, 176; benefits of,
  174–75; class plans in, 176–77;
  instruction notes in, 177–78;
  mission statement in, 175; quotes
  section in, 179; student/client
  notes in, 179; theme ideas listed
  in, 176, 179; values list in, 175;
  verbs list in, 180; vinyasa flows
  in, 179
teaching yoga: author's experience, 1,
  15–16, 31; benefits of, 271–72; as
  career choice, 2, 11, 53; challenges
  of, 10, 243; confidence with, 181;
  "container" for, 173, 241–42; creativity in, 67; current events in-
  tegrated into, 264–70; as lifestyle
  business, 8; money issues, 10–15,
  16, 31; passion for, 34; positive
  habits, 201–3; reasons for, 37–39;
  as relationship business, 159;
  rewards of, 7–8; scope of, 19; social media and, 149; sustainable,

60–62, 114–15, 116–20, 241;
  vicious cycle of, 15–16, 17. *See also*
  teacher training
teamwork, 112
tech problems, 103–6, 214
themes: arts/literature-related, 192;
  author's experience, 37, 131;
  chakra-related, 191–92; chance
  inspiration as source of, 193;
  class planning using, 173, 174,
  175, 176, 179, 182, 184–85, 188–96;
  crisis-related, 194–96; current
  events–related, 194, 224, 264–66;
  holiday-related, 193; introducing,
  202, 209, 221; mission statement
  and, 37; online series and, 82;
  postural, 191; pulsation-based,
  189–90; skilled teachers and,
  202; subscription model and,
  76; teacher insights as source of,
  190–91; theme-free classes, 196;
  for workshops, 52; yoga philosophy and, 188–89, 190
therapeutic applications, 17
Thinkific, 75, 82
Threads, 154–55
"Tigress, The," 245
TikTok: algorithm of, 152; business
  building on, 56; current popularity of, 137; format of, 152; infotainment on, 152–53; marketing
  on, 134; "population" of, 139; tips
  for using, 153–54; yoga creators'
  use of, 153; yoga students' use
  of, 141
time, as interdependent, 256–57
time management, 23, 51–52, 201, 241
timing, 31
training credentials, 108–9
travel concerns, 115–16, 117, 149, 233
trends, 150, 154
triangle pose, 208
tripods, 97
trust-building, 226
truthfulness, 236

union, 137
Union.Fit, 77, 79, 90

United States: business entity setup in, 166; genocidal beginnings of, 257–58; health insurance issues in, 167–68; social/environmental problems in, 251–53; yoga industry in, 12; yoga practice in, 8–9, 31
Uno, 28
utkatasana, 209

value propositions, 64, 65–66
values: business finances and, 165; business plan and, 108; class planning/preparation and, 175, 241; core, identifying, 30, 33–37, 40, 43; résumés or job applications and, 109; social media posts and, 144, 151; successful yoga teachers and, 30; as theme source, 264–65; of yoga students, 129; of yoga studios, 109, 110, 112; yoga values, 123, 264–65; yogins sharing, 1–2, 3, 9–10
Vedas, 261–62
Venmo, 79, 90
verbs, useful for teaching, 180
Vesselify, 3, 69–70, 184
vibration, 180
video cameras, 96
video conferencing, 69, 84, 89, 97. See also Zoom
video recordings, 200
videos, 142
video scripts, 233
vinyasa flows, 179, 212
vinyasa yoga, 177, 182–83, 216; miniflows, 179
violence, 251–52, 254, 270
virtues, yoga, 264–65
vīrya, 265
visibility, 88, 109–10, 144, 246
vision, 30
visual aids, 184
void, digital, 222–23, 227
volunteer work, 169–70
vulnerability, 27

Wanderlust, 70, 87, 127
warm-ups, 186, 201, 209

water element, 180
wealth gap, 252
web cameras, 73, 95
webinars, 73–74
websites, 82, 125, 127, 133
wellness, true, 255–56
wellness gap, 252
wellness industry, 69, 254–55
wellness publications, 135
West, the, yoga history in, 12–13
Westminster Kennel Dog Show (2008), 28
White, David G., 15
whitewashing, 254–55
wifi connection, 89–90
Wix, 77
Wizard of Oz, The, 192
women: pregnant, 52; as yoga teachers, 31–32
word of mouth, 90, 108, 138–39
workplace yoga, 56–58
workshops: balanced schedule including, 60, 61; building student base for, 52; business skills required for, 47; marketing funnel and, 125–26; marketing plan for, 133–34; online, 73–74, 77–79, 225–26; partner work in, 204

yamas, 24–27, 176
yoga, 8; alignment-based, 18, 200, 218; benefits of, 4, 7, 9, 123–24; differing styles of, 163, 203; eight limbs of, 25; fads in, 30; history of, 12–13, 18; hot flow, 30, 200; karma, xii, 263–64; life challenges and, 195; money and, 10–15, 123; as multifaceted education, 13; as pain/stress relief, 49; popularity of, 2–3, 8–9, 10, 30, 31, 71; restorative, 71; as sacred calling, 271–72; social networking and, 137; vinyasa yoga, 177, 182–83; workplace, 56–58. See also philosophy, yoga
Yoga Alliance, 8, 18, 109
yoga business channels. See business channels

yoga classes. *See* classes
YogaGlo, 70. *See also* Glo
"Yoga in America" report, 8, 43
Yoga International, 70, 87
"Yoga in the Digital Age," 253
yoga jargon, 203, 204–5
Yoga Journal (magazine), 8, 43, 169
Yoga Journal (platform), 70, 87
Yoga Journal Teachers (Plus), 169
Yoga Nidra, 71
yoga philosophy. *See* philosophy, yoga
yoga retreats. *See* retreats
yoga sequences. *See* sequences
yoga students. *See* students
yoga studios. *See* studios

Yoga Sutras of Patanjali (Patanjali),
    14–15, 24
yoga teachers. *See* teachers
yoga teaching. *See* teaching yoga
yoga tunnel vision, 162
"yoga voice," 221
yogins: author's experience of, 1–2; as
    grounded, 114; lifestyle cost for,
    114; marketing and, 122, 123, 126;
    social media and, 145–55, 151–52;
    tunnel vision of, 162; values of,
    1–2, 3, 9–10
YouTube, 70, 92–93, 197

Zelle, 79, 90
Zoom, 69, 79, 84, 89, 91, 95, 97, 233

About the Authors

Amy Ippoliti is known for making yoga accessible to modern-day practitioners in a genuine way through her intelligent sequencing, clear instruction, and engaging sense of humor. She shares her passions for conservation, climate justice, yoga, health, and food by writing for *Yoga Journal*, *Mantra*, *mindbodygreen*, and *Elephant Journal*. She has appeared on the cover of *Yoga Journal* and *Fit Yoga* and has been featured in *Self*, *New York*, and *Newsweek*. A graduate of Oberlin College and an ambassador for the Rodale Institute, Amy teaches on YogaInternational.com and at the Omega Institute, Esalen, and Kripalu. She has also taught at numerous festivals, including the Hanuman, Wanderlust, and Telluride Yoga Festivals. She is a pioneer of advanced yoga education and cofounded Vesselify (formerly 90 Monkeys), an online school that has enhanced the skills of yoga teachers and studios in sixty-five countries. Learn more at AmyIppoliti.com and Vesselify.com.

Taro Smith, PhD, is a movement specialist and a health and wellness entrepreneur. A graduate of the University of

Colorado, Boulder, where he studied integrative physiology, he has worked with many innovative organizations to make exercise and movement a standard part of care in the medical community. His research in the areas of exercise, aging, chronic disease, and immune function has been published in numerous peer-reviewed journals. He is also a certified yoga teacher who specializes in therapeutic yoga programs (for aging, pain, orthopedics, etc.) and yoga for sports. Taro has directed digital yoga and meditation content strategy for a variety of digital platforms, including Yoga International, Gaia, and Glo. Cofounder of Vesselify (formerly 90 Monkeys), Taro has presented at yoga conferences on career development for yoga teachers and spends his free time on marine conservation efforts, art, and photography. Learn more at Vesselify.com and TaroSmith.com.